Losing The Cybersecurity War

This book explains the five pillars or battlefields of cybersecurity and how a Zero Trust approach can change the advantage on each battlefield. We have taken a deep dive into each of five battlefields where we have a decided disadvantage due to constitutional structure and moral behavioral guidelines, and then provide examples of how we got here, what we can do about it, why we got here, and how we can avoid those traps in the future. This is a unique viewpoint that has never been explored – the five battlefields include Economics, Technology, Information, Education, and Leadership – and how each has contributed to our current disadvantage on the global stage. We go on to discuss how Zero Trust can change the game to create an advantage for us going forward. The credibility of Zero Trust stems directly from the father of Zero Trust, John Kindervag who says, "And now, Steve has written a new book on Zero Trust called: LOSING THE CYBERSECURITY WAR: Reversing the Attacker/Defender Dynamic on the Five Battlefields of Cybersecurity. It is undeniably the best Zero Trust book yet written. While other writers have focused on implementing Zero Trust from their perspectives, Steve focuses on why Zero Trust is so important on the modern cybersecurity battlefield. His concept of the five cyber battlefields is a great insight that will help us win the cyberwar. By weaving Zero Trust principles throughout these five concepts, Steve demonstrates how the ideas and efforts involved in building Zero Trust environments will lead to a profound shift in terrain advantage. No longer will attackers own the high ground. As defenders and protectors, we can leverage modern technology in a Zero Trust way to keep our data and assets safe from infiltration and exploitation."

Steve King is the Managing Director; CyberTheory and Founder/Executive Director, CyberEd.io; cybersecurity Expert certified CISM and CISSP. He has 20 years' experience in cybersecurity markets as CISO, CEO, and CMO; he is a Cybersecurity Technology Product and Services Sector founder and innovator; Digital Branding & Ad Agency founder, and his clients have included Starbucks, Matson, Abercrombie & Fitch, Harley Davidson, Lucky Brand, United Airlines, and Nike. He is a 3x Cybersecurity Start-up Founder and Exec, he has raised $40 million in VC, and he possesses multiple patents that encompass Remote Access MFA Authentication Methods Using Adaptive Machine Learning, an Actionable Cyber Threat Intelligence Network Platform, an Architecture for an IoT Cyber-Risk Platform, a Contextual Semantic Search Architecture, Web-enabled Multimedia Audio Transfers, and

Database Smart Query Processing. He is a former HealthCare and Computer Manufacturing CIO.

Kiren Chaudry is the product manager for CyberEd.io, the leading platform for cybersecurity education. Kiren's role is to manage the conversations and content across teams from marketing to course creation to platform development and drive the vision for the relaunch of CyberEd.io. In addition to her role, she loves grammar, language, obsessing over detail, and wearing the hat of part-time content editor. She earned her degree in Linguistics from Georgetown University and speaks English, Spanish, Russian, and dabbles in Arabic.

Losing The Cybersecurity War

And What We Can Do to Stop It

Steve King

Edited by
Kiren Chaudry

CRC Press
Taylor & Francis Group
Boca Raton London New York

CRC Press is an imprint of the
Taylor & Francis Group, an **informa** business

First edition published 2023
by CRC Press
6000 Broken Sound Parkway NW, Suite 300, Boca Raton, FL 33487-2742

and by CRC Press
4 Park Square, Milton Park, Abingdon, Oxon, OX14 4RN

CRC Press is an imprint of Taylor & Francis Group, LLC

ISBN: 978-1-032-36385-1 (hbk)
ISBN: 978-1-032-36408-7 (pbk)
ISBN: 978-1-003-33177-3 (ebk)

DOI: 10.1201/9781003331773

Typeset in Minion
by MPS Limited, Dehradun

Contents

Foreword

THE RAPIDLY CHANGING ECOSYSTEM OF DIGITAL connectivity has presented many challenges to industry, organizations, and government. At the top of the list has been cybersecurity. 2021 was one of the worst years ever in terms of cyber-attacks, exfiltration of data, and extorted funds from ransomware. This past year, critical infrastructure has also been under attack, including the vital assets of energy, water, healthcare, and transportation. Unfortunately, things seem to be getting worse in the efforts to mitigate cyber threats, not better. What has been lacking is the implementation of logical cybersecurity strategies and innovative ideas to keep us more cyber safe.

Thankfully, Steve King has authored an illuminating book that addresses past cybersecurity gaps and offers a pathway to true cybersecurity to help fill those gaps. In *Losing the Cybersecurity War*, Steve provides insights and remedies on what is needed to secure businesses, institutions, and individuals. It is a guidebook for both the CISO and anyone and everyone who uses a computer or smartphone in their daily lives.

Steve provides both definition and reasoning for a Zero Trust strategy model. Simply put, the breach statistics speak for themselves. The Internet was created for communication and sharing purposes without security in mind. As it expanded exponentially via cloud and edge and computing, the notion of defending the perimeter has become more challenging. There are more vulnerabilities (and targets) created every day with added devices and users, and attackers are taking advantage of our security predicaments. Zero Trust begins with the premise of implicitly not trusting any devices, assets, services, workflows, or people connected to the network. The next step is to assume everything connected is hostile and needs to be authenticated.

Employing a strategy of Zero Trust makes profound sense for improving cybersecurity fortification. It is already being widely adopted by the Pentagon and the Department of Homeland Security, and it is being mandated to other agencies via Presidential orders. The Defense Information Systems Agency (DISA) intends to implement a prototype for its Thunderdome Zero Trust architecture within six months. Zero trust is certainly on a fast track for government, and industry is likely to follow soon on that path as cyber-threats and the stakes for breaches keep growing.

Some of Steve's specific recommendations to reverse course and pursue a zero trust strategy are:

1. Change the reporting rules and prevent companies from reporting on their cyber- vulnerabilities;

2. Stop buying hardware made in China;

3. Implement central controls on Chinese venture firms;

4. Stop using any products or services, including mobile and telecom made in China;

5. Start sharing in earnest between public and private sectors;

6. Modernize our cyber-laws to enable offensive security;

7. Mandate a Zero Trust architecture and migration for every network within an aggressive time-frame,

8. Create and enforce national security mandates that specify technologies that must be part of every Zero Trust implementation,

9. Create the equivalent of a Manhattan project for the application of AI/ML to the problem space, with appropriate funding and speed to market; and

10. Implement mandates on insurance providers to match coverage against a standardized NIST framework requirement.

If we enacted those ten steps alone, cybersecurity would have new meaning and potency. While Steve highlights the urgent need and mechanisms for Zero Trust, his writing is really a field guide on how to meet and conquer current and future challenges in cybersecurity. Because cyber threats permeate every aspect of the converged digital/physical world, in addition to Zero Trust, other actions are required to holistically contain hackers and geopolitical adversaries.

You change the status quo by exploring past shortcomings and new paradigms. Steve does just that. The crux of his book is how the attacker–defender dynamics on five battlefields of cybersecurity can be reversed. Those battlegrounds are described as (1) Education, (2) Technology, (3) Intelligence (information) (4) Economics, and (5) Leadership.

In each one of those categories, Steve provides facts, anecdotes, and solutions. He also stresses that each of those battlegrounds needs to be a priority to an overall cybersecurity framework and mission. As an experienced cybersecurity practitioner with roots in government, corporations, and academia, I found his recommendation to be both instructive and imaginative. He understands and communicates the intricacies of the cybersecurity landscape and succinctly describes the roles (and potential) of policymakers and operators to improve it. He analyzes the strengths and weaknesses in his aforementioned five categories to redefine our cybersecurity postures and move forward to change the tables on how best to overcome our digital adversaries.

I particularly liked his discussion of emerging technologies for cybersecurity, especially the promising benefits that may be derived from artificial intelligence and machine learning. Such technologies can provide for more efficient decision making by prioritizing and acting on data, especially across larger networks with many users and variables. Emerging technologies will build an automation tool chest for horizon scanning technologies, analytics, audits, incident alert tools, diagnostics, and even self-repairing software. He caveats that we should invest in and develop emerging cybersecurity technologies, but we must be careful not to rely on "technology solutionism" as they are tools and correlate to needs and strategies. I wholeheartedly agree that elements of people and processes should be implemented congruently along with technologies for effective cybersecurity.

As I continue to teach cybersecurity risk management at the university level, I look forward to integrating *Losing The Cybersecurity War* into my curriculum. I will also use it as a research element in providing advice to companies and government clients. The book is comprehensive and in-depth for tackling the trying cyber issues that threaten us, both today and tomorrow. Although it provides sound technical advice that can be used by CISOS, CIOS, and CTOS, it also is easy to understand and follow for the non-expert reader. Steve's book is much more than a resource, it is a guide to a practical and systematic Zero Trust way forward for cybersecurity.

Chuck Brooks
Named Top Tech Person To Follow by LinkedIn
Named Top 5 Cybersecurity Exec to Watch
Georgetown U Faculty in Graduate Cybersecurity Program
2X Presidential Appointee
FORBES Contributor, Cybersecurity, Emerging Tech SME
teaches courses on risk management, homeland security,
and cybersecurity at Johns Hopkins University

Testimonials

S teve King's *Losing The Cybersecurity War* is a matter-of-fact look at where we have been and why we are where we are today in our cybersecurity journey. Steve lays out principles that can put us back on the right track as he explains the importance of Zero Trust. The principles are "The Five Battlefields of Cybersecurity": Education, Technology, Information, Economics, and Leadership. These principles will be meaningful for cybersecurity practitioners, corporate leaders, vendors, educational institutions, and our government. In each area, Steve offers opportunities for improvement.

> Education. Steve lays out the lengthy history of our attempts at teaching, but calls out where we fall woefully short, and where we should focus in preparing our cyber professionals. He also highlights what some of our adversaries do from a nation-state perspective and why they are so far ahead of us in the game.

> Technology. Steve points out how we're inundated with tech options and most organizations are spending significant portions of annual budgets on tech without commensurate results. AI and ML show promise. We should continue to develop and integrate this tech into our work. Leveraging Zero Trust into our design and implementations will improve the protection of our assets and data, reduce the overall attack surface, and have the potential to decrease breaches. I like where this is going. My own feeling is that all of this should be possible without breaking the bank and without spoiling the end-user experience. That said, overall implementation may require a phased approach to support budgeting, impact to resources, and implementation timelines.

Information. Information refers to information about the playing field. We need to know about our adversaries, their attack vectors of choice, technologies, and techniques. We also need to fine-tune how we use information and telemetry. Today, this intel is used by most of us to feed our defenses. Steve proposes we take on a more aggressive cyber posture and work together differently in the sharing of intel and vulnerability data.

Economics. Steve points out our security control costs to protect our systems and data far outweigh what it costs for the adversary to carry out attempted compromises. The economic factors are challenging and complex. Zero Trust offers a way out.

Leadership. Strong leadership from the CISO is important to setting the direction for the cybersecurity organization and for driving the somewhat opposed objectives with our IT partners. Again, Steve identifies a successful path forward by leveraging a Zero Trust strategy.

Tech and the threat landscape continue to change with faster networks and more interconnected devices. We must play a bit of catch up and change how we approach cybersecurity if we are to reasonably protect our most precious assets. Zero Trust isn't a single solution or roadmap to implementation. It likely means something different to all of us. Steve takes us through that journey.

In reading the book, I thought about architecture and design, selection of tech, implementation, and operations. I particularly liked the predictions and recommendations sprinkled throughout.

Steve, thank you for taking the time to put this into perspective and for your continued leadership.

Jackie Smith, Managing Director, Security Design at Charles Schwab

I enjoyed reading *Losing The Cybersecurity War* because it truly feels like a real battle these days and Steve really nails it. Each aspect of this book, especially these sections, resonates with me. The five battlefields are the subject of many passionate and often-unfinished discussions. Of the five, arguably the one topic that rises above the others is education. Education and intelligence sharing are the two keys to moving from the current state to a future state of cybersecurity that protects networks and data.

At a basic level, cybersecurity training should be taught just like math, spelling, and grammar. Recent events show how vulnerable our everyday lives have become. Each newsworthy outage, ransomware attack, and want from the Government and industry cyber leading companies stress the importance and the potential impacts of cyber threats. Massive amounts of technology exist purporting to protect one's network and data from compromise. At an expert level, no number of staff or technology can 100% prevent compromising a network. If we have learned anything from the last few years of experience, it will take leadership to address the Confidentiality, Integrity, and Availability of any company's desire.

Leadership starts with the Board of Directors (BOD) for publicly held companies and the CEO with privately held companies that have invested both in training itself and themselves on the threats that exist and in putting capabilities in play that will make companies more resilient. These groups need to be in continuous learning mode so they can address the challenges faced by being in an interconnected world; we need leadership that picks the right technology and uses all sources of information available to select and train a workforce that can quickly identify and remediate a threat.

Finally, we need to look at the role of the CIO as it relates to risk and the potential for conflicts of interest. Is the CIO the best leader to be in charge on this battlefield? Just like Audit reports directly to and is the eyes and ears of the CEO and CFO on the financial performance of the organization, so should be the role of the CISO. The CISOs' role has evolved to one of oversight and threat mitigation. Much like Sarbanes–Oxley bringing to light fraudulent financial practices, Boards and CEOs should be interested in bringing to light cybersecurity risks. The BOD and CEO need the raw visibility into the aspect of their organization that can take the whole company down in minutes.

This is an important read and contribution to a critical body of knowledge that every practitioner must have if they are to become part of the battle. Steve has built a compelling argument for all five pillars of the fight and Zero Trust as a solution that addresses every one.

I strongly recommend it.

Don Cox, CISO, American Public Education, Inc.
former CIO, Substance Abuse and Mental Health Services
Administration (SAMHSA)
ICE Director, and Special Internet Crimes Agent, U.S. Secret Service

Steve King's *Losing The Cybersecurity War* is today's far bigger lesson than Andy Grove's legendary book, *Only the Paranoid Survive*. King's book not only provides solid business operations advice, but elevates glaring white space void opportunities for entrepreneurs to fill and even more importantly underscores the existential threat to our vaunted corporations and institutions up to and including our country.

I strongly recommend a read – it is chilling.

Roger Lang, Partner, BCP Blitz Venture Capital
the Smart Society Fund, Bozeman, New York City, Oslo, Palo Alto

Steve has put together an excellent guide that explains the major differences in mindset between the traditional thoughts of cyber defense and marketing, and what the real world is like.

The illusion that we have been operating under where security can be thought of as something you can budget for and accomplish while minimizing expenses and keeping it away from the money-generating part of the business has been shattered by the activities of the last few years. He does an incredible job of discussing the significant challenges our adversaries pose, while juxtaposing them with the history of World War II and the Space Race as ones to be overcome, based on our history.

Instead of trotting out the same tired solutions meant to appease venture capitalists and their backers in China, Saudi Arabia, and other countries that have our demise in their interests, he proposes solutions that are realistic, achievable, and will get us to a better position if implemented. Instead of yet another white paper telling me to buy a certain product, Steve gives us a playbook to improve the industry as a whole and enable us to better protect all of us.

I strongly recommend a read.

CISO Mitch Parker, executive director of information security and compliance at Indiana University Health.

Losing The Cybersecurity War is a clarion call to change how we view the threat in cybersecurity and it provides an unfiltered lens on the impact to business, the economy, and geo-political risks that are relevant today and looking forward. Steve King's new book provides grounding for how we got into the current state of cybersecurity, but he doesn't linger there. Steve goes further and provides five key fronts in the battlespace that must be addressed in order to reverse the attacker–defender dynamic that persists today.

Losing The Cybersecurity War points out some of the obvious, as well as not so obvious failures in assumptions from a legacy of missteps in information security. Zero Trust is framed as the antitheist to excessive-trust ecosystems that have been exploited by expert and novice cyber-criminals alike. Open-source applications, open-ended attack surfaces, and third-party access to networks are just a few examples that Steve King points to. While these may seem obvious, it is the simple things done well that Zero Trust attempts to refocus the attention of security professionals on. The fundamentals matter and Steve adroitly points to five fundamentals to strengthen security going forward, yet he does so in such a way as to both educate and entertain at the same time.

You will not be bored.

Education, Technology, Information, Economics, and Leadership are foundational to reimagining the change that is needed. While it may appear to be a reframing of the same fundamentals, Steve takes a fresh look at each and identifies new ways to proactively improve security in the cyber battlespace. Steve does not rehash the same call to arms, he provides a new field-operating manual for rethinking cybersecurity. Fundamentally, the difference in success and failure will depend on how well we all recognize what has changed and respond accordingly. This is the subtle brilliance of this extraordinary book and I strongly recommend a read.

James Bone, Executive Director, GRCIndex
DBA, Cognitive Risk Institute
Advisory Board Member, CyberTheory
Lecturer in Discipline (former), Columbia University's S.P.S. School
ERM Program
Board Member, University South Florida MUMA Business School
Executive Cyber Program

Preface

D ECISIONS MADE IN THE CHAOS OF WARTIME OFTEN change the outcome of world history, but decisions must be made. Those who are gifted to choose at the fleeting intersection of courage and timing become heroes in the aftermath.

Those who are not, don't.

This is not intended to be a scholarly book, or a textbook for some college course on cybersecurity. This is simply my view of the global cybersecurity environment in which I have spent over 30 years building and integrating systems of defense against cyber-criminals and protecting information systems assets.

Much of what I have written here has appeared in various forms, like blog posts, white papers, and opinion pieces I have written over the last 10 years.

I mention this because it is an illustration that virtually nothing has changed in a decade of increased attention, spending, technology advances, education, and venture investment, all designed to improve our ability to counter our adversaries in cyberspace.

It could easily be argued that it not only hasn't changed for the better, but that it has gotten worse.

While we were doing all that, our adversaries have gotten better, smarter, more organized, creative, and sophisticated. Today's cyber-attacks make Stuxnet and Zero Days look like child's play. We now have complete affiliate marketing programs created by the Bad Guys around various forms of cyber-attacks, replete with money laundering, consulting, advertising, training, HR, and recruiting available on the dark web.

Our modern cyber-criminals operate largely out in the open, advertising their member programs and aggressively recruiting associates to pull the levers and tug on the strings for a piece of the action, ranging from 10% to 50%.

My thesis is that we are chasing our adversaries on five important battlegrounds:

1. Education

2. Technology

3. Intelligence (Information)

4. Economics

5. Leadership

Chasing means not leading.

If we don't catch up and soon, we will fall into the category of a third-world country, as least as it relates to cyber, and since we are the most connected country on the planet, the impact will resemble a Haitian hurricane.

China has made their position and consequences of interference from the West clear.

There will be no easy or even feasible way back.

In the wake of Nicolas Chaillan's resignation as the US Air Force's software chief and member of the Pentagon's security task force earlier this year, he told the Financial Times that "The US is far behind China on AI and we have no competing fighting chance against China in fifteen to twenty years. Right now, it's already a done deal; it is already over in my opinion."

Chaillan has gone on to say that the AI capabilities and cyber defenses of some US government departments were at the "kindergarten level".

So, the purpose of the book is to provide an easily consumable snapshot of where we are, where we've been, where we're going in Cybersecurity, and what we might be able to do about it by adopting the principles of Zero Trust on a global scale.

In plain English.

I hope it helps.

Acknowledgements

A lthough I am the named author of this book, it would not have been possible without the insights and advice, opinions, and thought leadership of people like John Kindervag, the creator and father of Zero Trust, my co-founder with the Cybertheory Institute and head of the Zero Trust council, a friend and trusted adviser who is graciously tolerant of my clumsy destruction of his design principles and framework, and Dr. Chase Cunningham, the Chief Strategy Officer of Ericom's Web Application and Remote Browser Isolation software aka the Doctor of Zero Trust, an early advocate and proponent of the Zero Trust strategy, having worked closely with John Kindervag at Forrester and with prior roles as a US Navy Chief Cryptologist who served at the NSA, CIA, and FBI.

Sam Curry, the CSO at Cybereason and former CTO and CISO for multiple cybersecurity vendors and market leaders and one of the smartest guys I know; Tom Kellerman, the Head of Cybersecurity Strategy for VMware Inc., a member of the Cyber Investigations Advisory Board for the United States Secret Service, a Global Fellow for Wilson Center's Global Fellow for Cyber Policy, and a clear thinker with unabashedly clear insights and opinions about change in the way we think about Cybersecurity; and Eve Maler, the rock-star CTO of ForgePoint, the co-creator of such landmark technologies as XML and innovating and leading standards such as SAML and User-Managed Access (UMA), a former Forrester Research security and risk analyst who served alongside John Kindervag, for her trust and commitment to our mission and her insights into identity management and privacy.

Richard Bird, the former CISO for PING Identity, and now, the Chief Product Officer for SecZetta, and as an internationally recognized data privacy and identity-centric security expert and global speaker, Richard has shed new light on some of the core aspects of Identity and has been a tireless and generous supporter both to me personally and to the cause of our Institute; Tony Scott, the newly minted CEO of Intrusion Cybersecurity, and a Senior Advisor for Cybersecurity and Privacy at Squire Patton Boggs, a prominent International law firm. Tony served in the Obama administration as the 3rd Federal CIO for the U.S. Government and is a senior fellow in the CyberTheory Institute.

You can't get better help than from CISO folks like Greg Touhill, Jeremy Grant, Kim Green, Summer Fowler, Roger Sels, Jackie Smith, Janet Bishop-Levesque, Toby Gouker, Jelena Matone, James Bone, and Don Cox.

A special thanks to Sheryl Root who allowed me to slip out of my commitment to teach at her amazing Carnegie Mellon University III program in Silicon Valley and for her support and council over years of friendship, my incredible team at CyberTheory with the mega-talented Julie Jordan competently multi-tasking under impossible deadlines and supported by the marketing brilliance of Lauren Geary and Larsen Lien, the design skills and original thinking of Caitlin Persichilli and Alexandra Perez and their willingness to work until it's done, the always above and beyond delivery through our genius data scientists Chase Anderson and Dan Fernandez, and most especially, the phenomenal Catherine Jermolowitz, without whom we would never have enjoyed as many satisfied clients as we have.

I also have the pleasure of working with Tom Field, the best cybersecurity editor on the planet and Mat Schwartz, probably the best cybersecurity writer/reporter in the field, who challenge us daily through their work discipline and results to do it better and deliver the highest quality work imaginable; Dave Elichman, the master of impossible events who single-handedly braved the pandemic over the last couple of years and brought highly successful, innovative, state-of-the-art virtual formats into the century; Dan Grosu, one of the least appreciated, yet most talented CTOs on the planet and his clarity about what needs to be done and what won't pass muster in software engineering; and to Varun Haran who runs a whole country for us and continues to be brilliant every day no matter what the topic within cybersecurity.

Extra-special thanks to our General Manager, Mike D'Agostino and founder/CEO Sanjay Kalra for their trust, patience, and support in encouraging us to continue bringing our unique CyberTheory story to ISMG's ever-broadening audience, along with the creation and supporting infrastructure for our CyberTheory Institute, whose mission is and will continue to be catalytic coalition of the best minds and thought leaders in the cybersecurity space bringing wisdom and creativity to the most difficult problems facing our new digital realities.

And I am most especially grateful to Kiren Chaudry, the remarkable and talented young woman who is responsible for getting everything delivered on time or under budget, whose skills at assimilating new and complex information and sorting it out through a thoughtful and creative presentation layer are unprecedented in my 100+ years in this business, and to whom I owe huge thanks for everything we've accomplished together.

Finally to my family – to my two sons and loving wife who have provided support and enthusiasm under the most difficult of circumstances, I will remain forever thankful and in debt.

Introduction

We awoke to the sounds of battle, but the world outside was still.

The thesis of this book is that we have made a flawed assumption about cybersecurity and based on that assumption, we have been investing heavily on people, processes, and technologies that are taking us in the wrong direction and causing us to lose the war against cyber-criminals and terrorists.

The results are clear and inarguable, and the evidence is irrefutable. The world spent more than $123 billion on cybersecurity in 2020, an increase of 9% from 2019 and, in addition, the federal budget for cybersecurity adds another $15 billion (that they can disclose publicly) to that spend rate. Yet in spite of that spending, in 2020, the number of data breaches in the United States came in at a total of 1001 cases (reported).

Meanwhile, over the course of the same year, over 155.8 million individuals were affected by data exposures – both record highs.

The cost of the average data breach to companies worldwide increased to $3.86 million (USD) while the cost of the average data breach to an U.S. company climbed to $7.91 million (USD) and the average time it took to identify a data breach rose to 196 days.

Every single metric points to an increase in successful cyber-crime, more breaches, new and improved malware and threat vectors, and increased spending to detect, prevent, and mitigate cyber-crime, breaches, and malware. (All data from Ponemon Research, Verizon, and ForgeRock studies.)

Net: We spend more each year and we get worse results.

If you are a consumer, you should assume that your data, and your biometrics, have already been confiscated and made available for sale on the deep or dark web. Following the Equifax breach, there are few Americans remaining whose data has not been stolen.

DOI: 10.1201/9781003331773-1

If you are a business, hospital, charity, airport, government agency, educational institution, or rely in any way upon the Internet, you should assume that you will be hacked, and your systems will be breached.

If you are a geo-politically conscious citizen, you should be worried that international cyber-strikes carried out by bad actors targeting America's critical infrastructure (energy, water, transportation, communication, and military grids) will be used as an alternative to kinetic conflict and will serve to escalate real-world tensions.

We are badly losing this cyber-war across all theaters of combat. From education to economics, from technology to intelligence, and from managerial approach to the psychology of engagement. This book will explain how and why and provide a recipe for success in each theater. But, not unlike every other war zone in the physical world, it will require critical thinking and practical rules of engagement.

Because when you are at war, you either decide to kill the enemy or the enemy kills you.

Earlier in my career, I ran large-scale data centers for a living – initially, a couple of local data centers for Memorex and later a national network of data centers for Health Applications Systems (HAS). Memorex manufactured large computer storage systems, communications peripherals, "mini-computers," and audio-cassette recording tape cartridges. HAS was the second-largest health-care claims processor behind Electronic Data Systems (EDS) at the time.

I mention these two companies because one of the themes in this book addresses the complexity facing today's Information Security practitioners, who are generally known as chief information security officers (CISOs). As you will see in this chapter, the role of the CISO may be the most difficult and challenging of all corporate governance responsibilities. Not only are they tasked with preventing cyber-crimes and data breaches which evolve daily and present as zero-day threats (those never seen before), but they must also do this work in disparate organizational cultures and technical environments protecting a broad variety of information asset classes.

In addition, just keeping abreast of the advances in technology and understanding their impact (5G, Blockchain, Zero Trust, etc.) on the computing environment makes for a long day with lots of distractions along the way.

Memorex thought of themselves as an innovative "fast" company, yet they ran conventional discreet and process manufacturing operations by today's standards, supported by conventional information technologies. Their secret sauce was innovative and supported by scads of patents but cranking out cassette tapes and digital storage systems was pretty mundane stuff and was framed in a fairly static organizational structure.

HAS, on the other hand, was driven entirely by a governmental and commercial contracting system that required new providers to be up and running within 90 days of the contract award with a data center presence located in the state in which the contract was granted. We opened new, behemoth data centers at such a pace that IBM had to continually knock other customers out of the queue in order to satisfy our needs (like Bank fo America, GM and Ford).

A pace that would have made heads spin at Memorex.

In addition, Memorex possessed digitized assets that reflected a deep library of patented chemical, engineering, and manufacturing processes representing high-value intellectual property while HAS instead held enormous volumes of what today is known as PHI – or personal health information – and other personally identifiable information on all of its customers' patients. The data vault at Memorex would not require regulatory compliance in today's terms, but the HAS data would have been protected under penalty of fine by HIPAA and other regulatory agencies at the state levels in 2021.

The processes involved in data protection and the cultural differences were like night and day and each required an entirely different set of skills and policies to succeed.

The CISO of 2022 is faced with a far more sophisticated and variable set of circumstances under which to manage and working with a complex set of moving parts in a static environment as it was in the Memorex and HAS days is nothing like managing the same moving parts in a dynamic and rapidly changing environment like the current world of cybersecurity. As you will see later in the book, running cybersecurity at the City of Atlanta is quite different than running it at Chase Bank.

I also served in the latter role for six years as CISO for the technology division of global retail banking for one of the world's top-three banks.

So, I know a bit about IT, OT, and cybersecurity.

In the middle innings of IT, running data centers also meant managing system programming teams.

System programmers were the glue that kept the early mainframe operating systems maintained, updated, and running properly. Which was necessary so that data centers could continue processing data without crashing. IBM owned the large-scale data center market at the time and their computing architecture was designed in such a way that the hardware and the operating system were separate components. This enabled IBM's customers to run various flavors of operating systems depending upon their needs.

A bug in the operating system that was not properly patched led to frequent and confusing outages, unhappy end-users, and a continuous dependency upon the system programmer.

System programmers worked in a language known as Assembler, which was a lower-level language than that used by programmers who built accounting and manufacturing applications in (which was usually) COBOL at the time. Lower level means closer to the operating system and thus much harder to learn and apply. System programmers were perceived to be the elite athletes or the "real" computer jockeys and were generally given a much looser length of rope than their counterparts on the business application programming side.

While at Memorex, I had the unique pleasure of "managing" one very smart young system programmer from the University of Michigan by the name of William (Shawn) McLaren. Shawn was able to solve the mundane daily challenges of keeping the operating system and associated software running with relative ease, which gave him plenty of time to think about larger issues like more efficient ways to utilize storage (disc) space and a better way to assure that sensitive data was protected from people who should not have access.

This thinking led to the development of an innovative storage space management capability, which led to Shawn's departure and to our creation of the Cambridge Systems Group, the commercialization of that storage archival capability and ultimately to the productization of a data security product known as ACF2, which quickly overtook IBM's competitive product (RACF) to become the market leader in that space.

ACF2 was arguably the first broadly successful data security product for the commercial markets and became the standard against which subsequent data security products were judged.

Even today, ACF2 is one of two market leaders in the data center security space.

Anyone running a main-frame data center at the time would recall their first meetings with the Internal Audit team who suddenly wanted to understand how all of this digital representation of information was being protected. It was the beginning of modern information security as

I knew it and while it would not be until 1994 when Citigroup suffered a series of cyberattacks from a Russian hacker and created the world's first formal cybersecurity executive office, staffed by Steve Katz, the world's first CISO, we had nonetheless embarked on the path toward consciousness about the protection of digital assets.

Back in those first few innings, none of my friends or former classmates understood what I did for a living. IT was (and remains today) a mystery to most people, including many CEOs who run large companies whose success depends increasingly on a digital world made possible through information technology innovation and management. IT was always perceived to be a dark dimension in which stuff happened that frequently resulted in reports being both wrong and late, systems crashing in the middle of the night, and the creation of mysterious worms and viruses snaking their way through the network and taking control over end-user terminals and workstations.

The fellow (as was almost always the case back then) who ran IT usually possessed a fairly shallow skill set focused on technology alone. Most people in corporate sort of kept their distance, as IT was recognized as a necessity, but no one knew how it did what it did or where to place it in the organization. Most often it reported to the CFO, which was a safe choice based on the premise that if you had something weird and too hard to understand, the safest place to put it would be with the finance guy.

That person who never loses anything and never lets bad stuff happen.

I mention this because as you will see, the evolution of today's CISO and the CIO roles and personality types along with their relationships within the organization have evolved through similar paths and present a formidable challenge to the business of getting cybersecurity right.

In the middle innings, that consciousness about the protection of digital assets got suddenly elevated through the adoption of a technology known as the Internet that, like the discovery and adoption of electricity, changed our world completely.

The Internet overnight enabled the connection of all computing devices on a global network that ushered in an era of access by anyone to anything and the exposure of new vulnerabilities, threats, and risk. The field that had been known as data security or information security was now being referred to as cybersecurity. It was one thing to protect information assets that were stored in a computer or on magnetic disc or tape and held in a secure data center facility whose access was controlled by physical security controls and armed guards.

It was something else entirely to protect those same assets now that they were out traveling deterministically through cyberspace.

It got really hard, really fast.

Threats suddenly spiked from the first computer worm created as a programming assist in the 1970s which was manipulated to destroy and alter data, to morph into a handful of self-modifying viruses in the 1990s. Following that 20-year span where the evolution of computer viruses went unaided by the Internet, came an onslaught of Microsoft Word-based viruses using macro commands that spread across the world, an epidemic of "Solar Sunrise" denial of service (DoS) attacks that successfully targeted hundreds of government, military, and private computer systems in the late 1990s to more advanced distributed denial of service attacks (DDoS) that crippled Amazon, Yahoo, and eBay's websites.

These multiple flavors of (D and DDoS) website attacks used a flooding technique to hammer the sites with so many requests that they ceased to function and crashed. In the DoS version, a single computer and one Internet connection is used to flood a targeted site. The more advanced DDoS attack uses multiple computers and Internet connections to flood the targeted site. I point this out because it is a classic example of how easily and rapidly bad actors can advance their art from one form of an attack vector to its next logical extension. DoS attacks became much more powerful DDoS attacks in under two years.

Fast forward to the next decade and by the mid-2000s, as the world connected to the Internet in unprecedented numbers, widespread infection rates exploded as well. In 2007, multiple advanced viruses were using email and social media platforms as spreading mechanisms, successfully infecting millions of computers. By 2009, sophisticated malware like Conficker and Heartbleed, which took advantage of vulnerabilities in security software libraries, were able to steal passwords, administrative credentials, and customer data.

In order to accommodate the Internet, computer software and operating system architecture evolved to provide logical interaction with the pipes that the Internet provided and in so doing, created a natural complexity with vulnerabilities that were easily exploited by bad guys. The first major breach that received global notoriety and caused the dismissal of the top IT and Information Security officers was the successful attack in 2013 on the Target Stores retail point-of-sale system servers that resulted in the theft of 70 million customer records.

And that seminal Target breach was quickly followed by an escalating string of ever-more advanced cyber-attacks over the last few years that have successfully hit big technology companies like Yahoo, Facebook, and Google; big financial services companies like CapitalOne, JP Morgan Chase, and Heartland; and big healthcare companies like Anthem, Banner, Blue Cross, and Community Health Systems. These have combined to represent hundreds of millions of sensitive personal health and other personally identifiable information to be stolen and offered for sale on the dark web.

As these threats evolved and multiplied, we in the cybersecurity industry found ourselves scrambling just to keep track of the techniques and technologies that were being used in each new breach and developing new software technologies, controls, policies, and processes as quickly as we could to prepare for, detect, block, and mitigate each new threat as it showed up in our environments. This reactive, responsive, and defense-oriented posture has been aptly described as a game of whack-a-mole.

If you have ever played or seen someone playing whack-a-mole, it becomes obvious immediately that no matter how many moles you hit on the head with your hammer, more moles will continue to appear. It is a comedic game played in the physical world only for laughs and only in arcades.

In the cyber-world, it is just as futile, yet promises a lethal outcome.

As I indicated in the beginning, as long as we continue to play this game by the rules established in the whack-a-mole world, we will continue to lose. We need to abandon the syllabus we have inadvertently created through our desperate requirement to respond and scramble to protect and defend as best we can and start moving toward a new doctrine that is focused on offensive, proactive risk management.

What does that mean and how will that change the shape of the problem space?

The book which follows identifies the current theaters of battle in which we prosecute this cyber-war, describes the ways in which we have fallen behind, and defines what must be done to reverse course. The battlefields are education, intelligence, technology, economics, and leadership.

In each theater, we are doing it wrong. And the more we continue doing it wrong, the more cyber-incidents, attacks, and breaches will occur, more records will be stolen, more data and identities will be manipulated, more lives will be placed at risk, and more of our intellectual and competitive advantage will be squandered.

As (retd.) General Keith Alexander, former head of the NSA; former commander of the U.S. Cyber Command; former chief of the Central Security Service; and founder, co-chief executive officer, and chairman of the board at IronNet Cybersecurity Inc., says, "We have to change the way we think about Cyber."

And that is our theme.

CHAPTER 1

What Is Zero Trust?

N ot a product or a service, nor a single component of identity or a network, Zero Trust is a reference architecture and strategy that, unlike traditional perimeter-based security approaches, enables an organization to achieve its objectives while adapting a security model that supports new-user populations, customer engagement models, rapid cloud adoption, and new IoT and OT devices and sensors.

What it does do is consume existing products and new technologies that serve the principles inherent in its architecture. It includes products from extended and unified endpoint protection, attack-surface visibility, threat intelligence, detection and response, SIEM, orchestration, micro-segmentation, MFA, identity access management, authentication and proofing, application security, and data loss prevention to SASE, SD-WAN, SOC-as-a-Service, cloud services, and network management and deception.

There is no question nor argument that we currently embrace broad excessive trust models for securing our networks, assets, services, data, and applications.

Our excessive-trust ecosystem allows one-time authentication, free-range network travel, an open-ended attack surface, and does not insist on exit authentication once sessions are ended.

Zero Trust reverses these processes so that we define a "protect surface" for small and manageable critical asset groups, segment that protect surface away from the network with microsegmentation technologies, assign policies at the level 7 application layer, require MFA for initial

DOI: 10.1201/9781003331773-2

access, and continuously monitor session behavior requiring repetitive MFA for subsequent requests as well.

The core principle of Zero Trust is to "never trust, always verify."

This ensures that not only are the right proxies allowed network access, it also ensures that the right proxies have the right level of access, to the right resources, in the right context, and that access is assessed continuously – so that we know that proxy accessing our payroll application is indeed Jennifer from Payroll who is in fact who she says she is.

But any journey toward Zero Trust must start small, grow incrementally, and achieve modest milestones while working to protect the business objectives before all others, and carving out a new architecture for future builds.

ADOPTER CHALLENGE

Zero Trust makes absolute sense on the surface, but the phrase has encountered some headwinds not uncommon in our business, especially today when every vendor is faced with a dozen competitors.

The more that point-solution vendors keep writing about how their solution will take us to the Zero Trust Promised Land, and the more they leverage the principles to drive product sales, the less credible the ZT model becomes as an evolutionary solution to most of today's cyber threats.

We are now in this log jam where the federal government has gotten on board by advocating for Zero Trust in a series of cyber-related executive orders, serious wards of IT and InfoSec in the private sector are in need of and curious about another, and better way to approach cyber defense, and on the other side, a marketing hype machine that has not only misrepresented Zero Trust but mangled it so badly, you wouldn't recognize it if it were sitting in your own driveway.

ZERO TRUST 24/7

One of our goals is improved education and communication. We believe the best way to break this log jam is to communicate clearly and often about Zero Trust, what it is and what it is not, and to conduct fireside chats with our founding members and interested third parties, where the case for Zero Trust can build itself.

This may take the form of participation at industry summits, round tables, speaking engagements, panel discussions, interviews and blog posts, white papers, podcasts, etc.

We plan on keeping Zero Trust alive in the news cycle, 24/7.

If a vendor has a product or service that contributes to the Zero Trust journey in a way that is useful, unique, and frictionless, we are happy to support it in any way we can. But, this effort is not intended to become a vendor bazaar, nor will we endorse products or services whose functionality toward Zero Trust is closer to a dream than reality.

We are and will remain completely vendor agnostic.

MISSION

The goal of Zero Trust is not to get to the point where we can say we have stopped 100% of all threats.

The goal instead is to shrink the attack surface, reduce our excessive trust landscape, and improve identity management with rigorous, always-on monitoring, and continuous insistence that our visitors can prove who they are and why they need access, thus elevating our confidence levels in whom we allow and/or disallow access, segment our critical assets away from the larger network, and make the bad guys' job much more difficult.

We believe that by doing so, we can seriously impact the quantity and depth of breaches, thwart ransomware and phishing attacks, and provide a much-needed respite from the assault while we determine the most effective way forward with emerging technologies like AI and ML that can primarily help us vs. the bad guys, in our defense against their constant incursion.

We believe that by enabling a majority of businesses and organizations to adopt these principles and begin the journey, we can gradually rotate the attacker–defender dynamic away from the asymmetric axis upon which it now sits and bring it closer into balance on both sides.

The journey to Zero Trust must be a pre-condition to operating a safe and secure IT environment, regardless of industry and organizational size.

Until all organizations begin to move toward Zero Trust, our interconnected world and supply chain implications will make it virtually impossible to operate safe and secure networks and eliminate launch pads for threat actors.

It is not that we don't know what to do, it's that we lack the will to do it.

CHAPTER 2

The Five Battlefields of Cybersecurity

EDUCATION

Education is the great chess game in the sky that when played with maximum intention, can catapult its heroes beyond the limits of the board, and into new dimensions of thinking and practice. When played poorly, the board actors may just as well have squandered their afternoons playing pool, drinking beer, and dreaming of what could have been.

We are relaunching our cyber-education platform very soon. It's called CyberEd.io, and will be chock full of educational content with guest lecture series by some of our biggest names, certification preparation for any and all possible certifications you can imagine, custom, leading edge training on topics ranging from Zero Trust to Critical and Design Thinking, and innovative security awareness training and cyber warrior training, mapped to the NIST/NICE working frameworks and all available under one trusted roof.

All taught by leading experts. All curated by leading CISOs.

Which is great, because our reach will guarantee that everyone in the cybersecurity space or adjacent functional roles, or even those just interested in cybersecurity will be able to have access.

Our goal is to close the gap between supply and demand for skilled, trained resources in cybersecurity.

And that gap represents one of the key challenges in our war.

DOI: 10.1201/9781003331773-3

Last year, Michigan's Davenport University announced it had received a five-year, $4 million grant from the National Science Foundation (NSF) to train and educate cybersecurity experts as part of its CyberCorps Scholarship for Service program.

That's nice for Davenport and Michigan, but it does virtually nothing to address the cybersecurity skills gap that we have created over the last 30 years by ignoring the threat and relying instead upon some kind of organic enthusiasm at the corporate level to balance out the demand.

This lack of national focus has resulted in 3 million unfilled cybersecurity positions as of 2021 and the US Bureau of Labor Statistics' predicts cybersecurity jobs will grow 31% through 2029, over seven times faster than the national average job growth of 4%.

Our enemies, on the other hand, have trained and developed tens of thousands of highly educated and skilled hackers who are, right now, creating new attack vectors, techniques, and technologies that they continue to employ to go after their commercial, industrial, and political targets mostly here in the United States.

North Korea is ironically, our most formidable adversary in education.

While many in Washington have continued to burn calories around a virtually non-deliverable NoKo nuclear threat, North Korea has been steadily developing their cybersecurity education programs. As a result of a committed and highly disciplined educational program, the North Korean cyber operations are more diverse, aggressive, and capable than any of our other enemies.

They are not just focused on espionage. Their warriors are perfectly skilled at sophisticated zero-day exploits, and at stealing vast amounts of IP from our most secured computer networks even when they are air-gapped and isolated from the internet, for example, military servers and power plant control systems.

These North Korean attackers have been trained in measuring electromagnetic radiation leakage from air-gapped computers and extracting critical data after only a few seconds of monitoring.

This is not a course we teach at any cybersecurity graduate program in the United States.

In the early 1990s, when computer networks were beginning to reach a level of maturity, a group of North Korean computer scientists proposed a massive educational program to teach advanced cyber-espionage and cyber-hacking with the goal of graduating 10,000 student hackers by the year 2015. To qualify for entry into these programs, applying students had to demonstrate not only outstanding academic ability, but also the ability to read, write, and speak flawless English.

It was the North Korean equivalent of India's IIT in terms of how difficult it was to gain entry.

While they were doing that, we were offering cybersecurity degrees at 17 universities that same year. Today, we offer rated cybersecurity degrees at over 65 universities, but the curricula are all centered on or around standardized frameworks for cybersecurity defense or focused on basic criminal forensics.

They are not grounded in warfare.

Undergraduate course offerings on subjects like fundamentals of computer troubleshooting, network security, ethical hacking, Windows server: install and storage, Linux system administration, etc., indicate that the intention is to graduate a system admin or network admin with a BS degree in Computer Networks and Cybersecurity.

This is the baseball equivalent of bringing in a minor league class A ball player to pitch to Aaron Judge, with the bases loaded.

Graduate course offerings like those offered by one of our leading universities include foundations of cybersecurity, applied cryptography, secure systems architecture, cybersecurity risk management, cybersecurity operational policy, management and cyber security, secure software design and development, network visualization and vulnerability detection, cyber intelligence, cyber incident response and computer network forensics, etc.

Opening the syllabus for these courses reveals that all of the content can be found in industry certifications like CISSP, CISM, CEH, and CRISC, which can be obtained quickly and easily at a fraction of the cost of that University's Master's Degree in Cyber Security Operations and Leadership. Now maybe there's some magic in how the professor guides students through the material, but if the goal as stated is to "equip students to stay abreast of ongoing changes in threat and mitigation as lifelong learners in the field," the coursework falls far short.

Particularly in a remote learning world like the one we now find ourselves.

What we need instead is coursework centered on actual red-team tactics across a full range of cyber-weaponization. We need well-trained cyber-snipers and military-grade penetration rangers who can throttle through the most advanced and sophisticated defenses and commit the greatest possible damage in the least amount of time. Our flimsy educational offerings in cybersecurity seem intended to graduate future administrators and bureaucrats when our greatest deficiency is in the working warrior classes.

Pushing North Korea's cyber educational units to dramatically level up in capability, Kim Jong-un proclaimed, "Cyber warfare is an 'all-purpose sword' that guarantees our military's capability to strike relentlessly."

In stark contrast, it seems the actual goal of our own university programs can be found in one of that university's program descriptions where their stated purpose is "to collaborate with important stakeholders in the cyber security community to explore ways to keep the curriculum immediately relevant and to assist in the placement of our graduates."

This assessment is in no way intended to denigrate the competent and well-intentioned professionals who conceive and guide these programs at these really good schools. The problem is the coursework contains nowhere near the information or education necessary to either create an advanced attack vector or defend against today's sophisticated cyberattacks.

The curriculum is way too generalized. The syllabus is too lightly challenging. The objectives are too easily achieved, and the graduating students are no more prepared to join the battle than if they had simply been working as a network administrator for a few years in any IT department in America.

We will not win this war with this level of training and education. We need a moon-shot and the impetus for a program of that magnitude must come from Washington. Unfortunately, there are no signs of anything of that nature appearing on anyone in Washington's to-do list.

And that is a problem.

It's a problem because a little country like North Korea has emerged as a significant and serious cyber threat to the United States, with an army of over 10,000 highly trained warriors honing their skills with hundreds of practice attacks on a variety of targets around the world. The probes we see on our own critical infrastructure targets are warnings of future attacks against which we are incapable of defense at our current levels of preparedness.

Our response?

In an attempt to ignite some movement of the cybersecurity education front, we created an organization in 2008 that was designed to make the Federal cybersecurity workforce better prepared to handle cybersecurity challenges. The National Initiative for Cybersecurity Education (NICE) is a partnership between government, academia, and the private sector focused on supporting the country's ability to address current and future cybersecurity education and workforce challenges through standards and best practices. NICE is led by the National Institute of Standards and Technology (NIST) in the U.S. Department of Commerce.

Our department of Homeland Security (DHS) has partnered with not-for profits, middle and high schools, universities, and State school boards across the country to help incorporate cybersecurity concepts into our nation's classrooms. DHS is also partnered with the National Integrated Cyber Education Research Center (NICERC) to provide K-12 cybersecurity curricula and hands-on professional development for teachers at no cost. DHS claims the grant has helped get their cybersecurity curricula into the hands of over 15,000 teachers impacting 820,000 students in 42 States. The curricula is focused on subjects like Cyber Fundamentals, Algebra I, and Computational Thinking.

But the important idea here is that it is offered to public school teachers along with grant money that might encourage engagement yet completely without regard to qualifying student interest. It falls right into the civics or history buckets, where the natural question for an 8-year-old is why do I need to know this, and how will it affect my life?

STEM is great if you are interested in STEM. If you're not, then not so much.

DHS and The National Security Agency (NSA) jointly sponsor the National Centers of Academic Excellence (CAE) program, designating specific two- and four-year colleges and universities as top schools in Cyber Defense (CD). Schools are designated based on their robust degree programs and close alignment to specific cybersecurity-related knowledge units (KUs), validated by top subject-matter experts in the field. CAE graduates help protect national security information systems, commercial networks, and critical information infrastructure in the private and public sectors.

To encourage students to enter cybersecurity degree programs, DHS co-sponsors the CyberCorps: Scholarship for Service (SFS), providing scholarships for bachelors, masters, and graduate degree programs focusing in cybersecurity in return for service in Federal, State, local, or tribal governments upon graduation. The scholarship assists in funding the typical costs incurred by full-time students while attending a participating institution, including tuition and education and related fees. The scholarships are funded through grants awarded by the National Science Foundation (NSF) in partnership with DHS and the Office of Personnel Management (OPM).

It turns out, however, that students have an obligation to re-pay the scholarship in service to a State, local, tribal government organization, or Congressional agency upon graduation and they must commit to a three–four-year service term depending on their scholarship funding. A graduate will be hired as a G9 at a pay rate of $23/hr. and if you don't like that wage so much, you can refund the entire scholarship amount. The entire program was funded with $25 million in 2018, which is about the same amount we spend on food stamps for dead people in New York and Massachusetts each year (not a joke).

We continue to try and innovate at the Federal government level bound by 50 year old process and procedural rules - it doesn't work!

Workforce shortages exist for almost every position within cybersecurity, but the most acute needs are for highly skilled technical staff.

Nine years ago, a Center for Strategic and International Studies (CSIS) report entitled "A Human Capital Crisis in Cybersecurity" found that the United States not only has a shortage of the highly technically skilled people required to operate and support systems already deployed, but also an even more desperate shortage of people who can design secure systems, write safe computer code, and create the ever more sophisticated tools needed to prevent, detect, mitigate, and reconstitute from damage due to system failures and malicious acts. At the time, we only had about 1000 security specialists with skills and abilities to take on these roles, compared to a need for 10,000 to 30,000 professionals.

In 2016, CSIS found that IT professionals still considered technical skills like intrusion detection, secure software development, and attack mitigation to be the most difficult to find skills among cybersecurity professionals.

A 2018 survey revealed that a lack of required technology skills was one of the greatest challenges facing organizations when hiring cybersecurity candidates. These challenges were particularly acute for mission critical job roles, with over a third of organizations reporting a lack of technology skills for vulnerability assessment analyst positions and half of employers reporting deficiencies for cyber defense infrastructure support candidates.

What follows is the brief yet remarkable history of the Federal government's attempt at closing the skills gap:

In May 1998, a presidential directive was signed by Bill Clinton requiring that the Executive Branch assess the cyber vulnerabilities of the Nation's critical infrastructures; information and communications, energy, banking and finance, transportation, water supply, emergency services, and public health, as well as those authorities responsible for the continuity of federal, state, and local governments. The directive also called for the Federal Government to produce a detailed Plan to protect and defend America against cyber disruptions.

This National Plan for Information Systems Protection was the first major draft of a more comprehensive effort to protect our nation's critical infrastructure.

In 2000, The CyberCorps® Scholarship for Service Program (SFS) was created under the Federal Cyber Service Training and Education Initiative, a component of the National Plan for Information Systems Protection, Co-Sponsored by National Science Foundation and Department of Homeland Security, to enhance the security of critical information infrastructure, increase the national capacity of educating IT specialists in Information Assurance (IA) disciplines, produce new entrants into the Government IA workforce, increase national Research & Development (R&D) capabilities in IA, and strengthen partnerships between institutions of higher learning and relevant employment sectors.

In 2001, the first grants were awarded to four schools and the first graduating class made up of nine students entered the Federal IA workforce in 2002.

In 2014, more than 16 tears after the Clinton directive, the Cybersecurity Enhancement Act of 2014 was signed into law (Public Law No: 113–274). Its stated intent is to provide for an ongoing, voluntary public–private partnership to improve cybersecurity, and to strengthen cybersecurity research and development, workforce development and education, and public awareness and preparedness.

It also reflects the critical need for Information Technology (IT) professionals, industrial control system security professionals, and security managers in Federal, State, local, and tribal governments. The SFS program is managed by the National Science Foundation (NSF), in collaboration with the U.S. Office of Personnel Management (OPM), the Department of Homeland Security (DHS), and in accordance with the

Cybersecurity Enhancement Act of 2014 (Public Law No: 113–274). Section 302 of the act addresses the SFS program specifically.

In 2018, the National Defense Authorization Act of Fiscal Year 2018, mandated SFS program updates and enhancements, among them the requirement that students identified by their institutions for SFS Scholarships must meet selection criteria based on prior academic performance, likelihood of success in obtaining the degree, and suitability for government employment.

Since the inception of the program in 2001, approximately 3600 SFS graduates have found placement in more than 140 government entities, or roughly 1% of the projected U.S. InfoSec job openings by the end of this year.

What organizations are truly desperate for are graduates who can design secure systems, create new tools for defense, and hunt down hidden vulnerabilities in software and networks. None of these skills are being taught in any of the coursework that we find in the Davenport University Cybersecurity program.

Russia and China have been running rigorous cybersecurity educational programs for years and have trained upward on 100,000 cyber-warriors. As a result, both countries possess the highest levels of technical sophistication, far more advanced than the United States.

China has moved into the lead position in Quantum Computing having even installed their own Quantum-based communication system between Beijing and Shanghai.

Both China and Russia have demonstrated competency in full-spectrum operations, including the ability to coordinate the capabilities in cyber-operations with the other elements of state power, including conventional military force and foreign intelligence services that have global reach. Their exhibition of cyber-attack prowess demonstrates the potential to cause complete paralysis and/or destruction of an adversary's critical systems and infrastructure, resulting in significant destruction of property and/or loss of life.

Under those circumstances, regular business operations and/or government functions cease, and data confidentiality, integrity, and availability are completely compromised for extended periods, including forever.

For an example of how good the Russians are at this stuff, consider the average amount of time it takes for a Russian cyber-attacker to conduct a "breakout" which is the act of leaving the entry beachhead and moving laterally within the network to prepare for an attack. The gold standard for detection, investigation, and remediation in the cybersecurity industry is what is known as the 1-10-60 rule and only the best and most prepared businesses can manage it.

It translates to detection within one minute, investigation within ten minutes, and remediation within one hour (60 minutes). The Russian average breakout is 17 minutes with the fastest recorded as low as seven minutes. Today's best prepared businesses in cybersecurity defense terms will never catch a Russian intrusion in time to prevent damage.

This threat is very real and very present, yet we continue to ignore it both at the state level and within all public and private businesses.

In response to this incredible imbalance in capabilities, we make a childlike political gesture of outlawing the best cybersecurity research on the planet from use by federal agencies because it is headquartered in Russia (Kaspersky).

Then to apparently be sure we are fully cooperating with our adversary's advancement in cybersecurity capabilities, we encourage their participation in U.S. investments and welcome Chinese venture capitalists and their LPs into our startup eco-system and allow them to take a large enough position in AI/ML cybersecurity ventures where they become entitled to unfettered access to the venture's IP.

That access goes right to the Chinese ministry of National Defense because nothing happens in commercial markets without the Chinese government's approval and control. There is no such thing as an independent business in China. As the former CTO and CISO of a Cybersecurity Systems Integrator doing business in China for seven years, I can assure you that all Chinese businesses, including venture capital firms in the United States, are by proxy, acting as Chinese government agencies.

The Worldwide Threat Assessment of the U.S. Intelligence Community is a document published each year, which itemizes the significant threats to the United States and its allies. This year's report claims that China and Russia pose the greatest espionage and cyberattack threats to the United States but also warned that other adversaries and strategic competitors like Iran and North Korea will increasingly build and integrate cyber espionage, attack, and influence capabilities into their efforts to influence U.S. policies. It warned that rivals to the United States are successfully developing capabilities to "shape and alter the information and systems" that the United States relies on.

And, on a daily basis, as we connect and integrate tens of billions of new digital devices into our lives and business processes, adversaries, and strategic competitors will be able to gain even greater insight into and access to our protected information. In particular, the report warned that China and Russia present a "persistent cyber espionage threat and a growing attack threat" to U.S. core military and critical infrastructure systems, businesses and social media, as well as attacks designed to aggravate social and racial tensions, undermine trust in authorities, and criticize perceived anti-Russia and anti-Chinese politicians.

In summary, we don't have enough educational programs, the ones we do have are focused on the wrong skills and the degrees are too easily obtained. A degree in Cybersecurity isn't like a degree in Political Science where the assumption is that the student will learn how to apply the training once engaged with real-world dynamics, through mentors and the process itself. Or a degree in Physics, where the application of the training will be relevant immediately because the rules that govern the domain haven't changed in a hundred years.

Cybersecurity changes every minute and the real-world realities have little to do with our current curricula.

Additionally, we have insufficient national emphasis on cybersecurity education and at the highest levels of government we fail to recognize or acknowledge the severity of the threat. Instead of making progress over the last decade we have regressed dramatically.

The attacker–defender dynamic in education has become even more asymmetric and the gap between what is necessary, and the state of our current skill base has expanded even further.

Look. I get it.

Our four principal adversaries operate within totalitarian government structures and can dictate whatever form of education their leaders deem necessary for national defense. And I certainly am not arguing for America to adopt any of those characteristics. On the other hand, I see nothing wrong with the declaration of a national emergency and the organization of a Manhattan-like (or of you prefer a Moon-shot) project that could transform a volunteer army into a competent cyber-defense military unit who could operate within a new set of rules for the engagement of a clear and present enemy.

Here's a proposal:

Let's spend $30,000,000 in new tax-payer dollars on a National Cybersecurity Masters Education program where we invite 500,000 college graduates with undergraduate degrees in engineering, math and science to participate in a fully funded, 2-year graduate program focused on building cyber-warrior skills. When I say fully funded, I mean $40,000 in tuition and $20,000 in living expenses each year. The entrance requirements would be similar to any graduate degree program in Engineering, Law or Science at any leading University. Upon graduation, these students would be free to do what they want. Most would pursue a job in private industry. Some would become civil servants. Others may abandon the profession altogether.

But we will have created a fast program that highly incentivizes participants, removes all reciprocal restrictions on post-graduation service and has a high probability of success.

The best part is that it will cost each U.S. taxpayer exactly $209.79. That is what we spend on a cable TV subscription for one month. Let's get even crazier and throw in a $20,000 recruiting fee to help the graduates find a great job upon graduation. That will cost another $1.40 each.

$12.58 per year.

That math is powered by 143 million taxpayers in 2020.

A simple program like this, with origins in Zero Trust thinking, run by our public and even private University systems, and not under the auspices of any government agencies, could quickly close the skills gap and flood hundreds of thousands of future CISOs and skilled Cyber-warriors onto a thirsty market. Instead of bureaucrats and administrators, this brand of CISO would be trained in hand-to-hand cyber-enemy combat and equipped with the appropriate tools necessary to take the fight to the enemy, shifting the attacker–defender dynamic to offense and away from detect, respond, and remediate.

We should supplement that with a purpose-driven Cybersecurity education and training program that is offered on a just-in-time basis on-line, and delivered through a modern platform designed with the user experience as the top priority.

A program that has been vetted by CISOs and not a bunch of cybersecurity practitioners who drive curriculum creation through a necessarily narrow view of the landscape owing to their limited prior experience.

A program that delivers all levels of training, for cybersecurity practitioners, engineers, analysts, CISOs, non-CISO executive suite, and board members, along with everyone else in an organization in a curated context that will insure everyone is getting exactly what they need, when they need it and in a consumable, consistent and repeatable set of programs overseen by an assigned success manager who assures that value is continuously extracted and applied.

An online learning program designed to be an extension of an organizations' expanding purview over Cybersecurity education, delivery, absorption, and execution.

A program unlike any other on today's commercial markets, and one in harmony with NIST guidelines and the NICE framework that, in addition to preparing students for certification exams in over 150 specialties, can also bring outer-dimensional thinking to the creation and building of new cybersecurity architectures and programs like Zero Trust, designed to move away from traditional, heritage programs and toward those best suited for modern cyber-warfare.

Because we all now live in a digital world and cannot continue to ignore our individual responsibilities to manage our digital environments with dutiful care, it has been recommended that, in addition to the earlier described solutions, a model for a National Cybersecurity Service (NCS) program be mandated as a two-year public service requirement for every college graduate in the country – a war-time peace corps – less than half the service requirement for graduates of Annapolis – and/or 18-year olds who want to pursue a career path in Cybersecurity without attending college.

The Israeli's didn't manage to survive all these years by pretending their enemies were their trading partners. In much the same way as the Israeli Defense Forces (IDF) accommodates varying interests, our own NCS would offer different specialty educational opportunities, but the program concentration would be on a warrior-level and offensive cyber training.

Framed as a Manhattan project, such a program can be both authorized and funded by Presidential order (ala FDR) and Congressional mandate (though many would question whether any recent Congress would have either the political appetite or courage to do so). Regardless of cost, it would likely be dwarfed by legislation that we push through our law-making process on a daily basis and would be the only initiative aimed directly at a true existential threat, and one acting as a clear and present danger, and not just a measurable, abstract probability ten years into the future.

But if we don't do something really soon, it won't matter how many new technologies we invent, how much new cyber-threat awareness we create in our corporate boardrooms or how many new initiatives we create around the traditional approaches to managing cybersecurity. If we don't shift our approach to a risk management model, re-build our cyber-defense infrastructure on the basis of a Zero Trust architecture, and staff it with an abundance of trained warriors, we will continue to retreat from this cyber-war front in the business of business, out-resourced, out-smarted, and out-intimidated by opposing forces un-encumbered by layers of social justice and political correctness, just as we have been doing for the last 20 years.

And at a national security level, it won't matter how many sub-marines, aircraft carriers, jet fighters, or other military hardware and human resources we can muster against our enemies in some conventional theater of war either.

The next International war will be fought in cyber-space and right now, things don't look too good for the U.S. team.

"Cybersecurity's response to bitter failure, in any area of endeavor, is to try the same thing that didn't work ... only harder."

~ Marcus Ranum, an early developer of the first commercial bastion host firewall and the first Internet email server for the whitehouse.gov domain, who also is the author of the eponymous Ranum's Law, "You can't solve social problems with software."

TECHNOLOGY

The first major technologies were tied to survival, hunting, and food preparation. In 2.5 million years, nothing has changed.

The thesis is simple: We have too much, it's the wrong kind, and it does us little good.

I know I just made about 3500 enemies. One of each of the 3500 product vendors in the cybersecurity space, but if we are to be honest about our present state, it would be hard to argue that we don't have enough technology.

Wouldn't it?

I am a huge fan of technology and all of the vendors in this space. My entire orientation throughout my IT career has been on the technical and operational side. My cybersecurity experience has always been in the trenches, analyzing, assessing, and remediating. I have worked with teams of bankers and industry leaders on process, compliance, and audit, but my interest and passion are in technology.

So, when I ask how many SIEMs does it take to screw in a lightbulb? How many EDR products? How many Firewalls, Network Behavioral Analytics tools, anti-virus offerings, vulnerability management platforms, threat intelligence feeds, etc.? It is about having seen so many of these products at work, demonstrating their strengths and weaknesses, that when I hear about a new product or even service in the space, my initial reaction is dis-belief and skepticism like most every other CISO I know.

BeyondTrust, Thycotic/Centrify, One Identity, and CyberArk all make a great Privileged Access Management product, so do we really need 20 other leaders, challengers, niche players, and visionaries in the Gartner Magic Quadrant for PAM? Fortinet makes the best SIEM product on the market. Do we need another 18 vendors? Have any of these Gartner-approved solutions solved for data breaches?

Based on the available statistics, they apparently have not.

Does anyone pay attention to Gartner anyway? Everyone in the industry pretty much understands that if you are a large-check-writing Gartner customer, you kind of get to call the shots as to how you are labeled and positioned and in which quadrant you get placed, right?

Small check writers, not so much.

How is this a legitimate industry analysis? And, what do actual end-users think about all these products? You know, like CISOs?

Who knows?

Why?

Because no one asks them. Instead, the insurance industry has decided that through the Marsh brokerage unit of Marsh & McLennan Cos., a group of insurers will evaluate cybersecurity software and technology sold to businesses, collate scores from participating insurers, and with the assistance of (wait for it) ... Microsoft, they will identify the products and services considered effective in reducing cyber-risk. Yes, this is the same Microsoft that recently disclosed a waterfall of vulnerabilities across its product line.

Everyone is susceptible, but asking a leading technology vendor with a poor record of cyber-defense in its own product suite to sit in judgment over other vendors' efficacy in reducing cyber-risk seems a bridge too far to me.

The theory behind this plan is that a collaborative effort across many insurers has a better chance of bringing to light weak cybersecurity products that should be avoided by manufacturers in global supply chains.

Called "Cyber Catalyst," the Marsh initiative focuses on offerings that address risks such as data breach, business interruption, data corruption, and cyber extortion. They include technology-based products such as firewalls and encryption, tools for monitoring threats, and training and incident-response planning.

In addition to the over-abundance of redundant technologies, none of which appear to be capable of stopping cyberattacks, we have an asymmetrical disadvantage in the attacker–defender dynamic. The attacker has at its disposal, the very latest pre-programmed kits and techniques available both as software agents and as a service that can be used to penetrate and disrupt our latest defenses.

We, in turn, develop new defense techniques whose effectiveness increases rapidly until it reaches a level of effectiveness that prompts adversaries to respond.

Attackers quickly discover ways to evade the defensive technique and develop countermeasures to reduce its value. That is the cycle we have been stuck in for years.

Good for attackers. Bad for defenders.

In the meantime, we have just expanded our threat landscape through an almost universal embrace of an ideology called "technological solutionism." This ideology is endemic to Silicon Valley and it reframes complex social and technical issues as "neatly defined problems with definite, computable solutions … if only the right algorithms are in place!"

This highly formal, systematic, yet socially and technically myopic mindset, is so pervasive within the industry that it has become almost a cartoon of itself. How do we solve wealth inequality? Blockchain. How do we solve political polarization? AI. How do we solve climate change? A blockchain powered by AI. How do we solve cybersecurity attacks? A blockchain powered by AI with some advanced predictive analytics and a little machine learning.

This constant appeal of a near-future with perfectly streamlined technological solutions distracts and deflects from the grim realities we presently face. You need only attend one RSA conference to grok that reality.

The pre-eminent cybersecurity conference on the entire planet has degenerated into a carnival atmosphere with barkers, cash-giveaways, side-shows, dancing girls, skimpily clad booth hostesses, and serious booze parties.

Not a critique, just reality – I fully understand the challenges of attracting potential buyers to your pitch amid the noise and chaos of 3500 competitors – one must do something.

But if you just dropped in from Mars, you would conclude that cybersecurity is an annual comedy event where 3500 vendors participate in the art of inflated promises, hard-ball sales tactics, cherry-picked customer success stories, collusive relationships with a handful of leading industry analysts, supported by equally skimpily clad evidence of success, all culminating with a crazed, super-bowl party in February in San Francisco.

Given our recent bout with the pandemic, it is likely that attendance will be substantially down in coming years, providing cover for marketers who don't believe that the customer acquisition cost justifies the spend – and we are blind to the probability of a return to normal or when that may happen.

Rendering trade shows a risky expense.

It turns out that a joint research tool created by CNN and Moody's, the Back to Normal Index reached 92% as of mid-year 2021. This analytic scale—which touches on many aspects of life in America—set "normal" at 100, representing how things were going in March 2020.

A return to normalcy includes a return to business as usual and the consideration of trade shows as a potentially enduring source of new business generation in America.

The index is made up from consumer credit scores, unemployment claims, job postings, air travel, and hotel occupancy data—and attempts to be a barometer of recovery.

Ninty-two percent implies we're almost there, but that last mile may be a little tricky – working from home is now accepted and expected, geographically dispersed workforces are now normalized, and while enthusiasm for vacation travel is high, that may be factoring into the air travel data in misrepresentative degrees.

Finally, we are not out of the COVID woods yet.

Data suggests that the B2B trade show market in the United States was worth 15.58 billion U.S. dollars in 2019 and took a massive hit in 2020, dropping 75% in value. If the events markets were the pathways for new solution vendors to enter competitive spaces, then the prospects for recovery look grim in years to come, as industry analysts don't predict a return to 2019 levels for five more years.

What do trade shows have to do with technology?

Unfortunately, a lot.

For example, AI dominates current technology discussions from boardrooms to venture capital LP meetings, to CISO conferences, and the State department. China continues to march far ahead of us in AI and ML technology, having stolen much of it from our own technology startups, and has developed quantum solutions we are still trying to understand. What do we do instead of developing our own quantum capabilities? We haul folks like Zuckerberg in front of Congress and get his promise to develop better AI for content moderation.

But AI remains the tent-pole of the cybersecurity technology framework today. The now-old joke continues that if you want to raise VC for your cool new cybersecurity whatever, make sure you include about 25 references to AI throughout your pitch deck.

To build cyber defenses capable of operating at the scale and pace needed to safeguard our information assets, artificial intelligence (AI) could be a critical component in the tech stack that most organizations can use to build a degree of immunity from attacks. Given the need for huge efficiencies in detection, provision of situational awareness and real-time remediation of threats, automation, and AI-driven solutions should be major contributors to the future of cybersecurity.

By efficient, we mean AI-based solutions that automate human analysis and then substitute in real-time, replacing a security analyst team for more accurate results.

We are not there yet.

And as we have seen, the cybercrime data to-date is evidence that any technical developments in AI are quickly seized upon and exploited by the criminal community, posing entirely new challenges to cybersecurity in the global threat landscape.

One weakness of machine learning models is that they require constant supervision to avoid becoming corrupted, which is something the bad guys manage to do. The use of AI and ML in detection requires constant fine-tuning, and AI has yet to invent new solutions to security problems; its principal value has been in doing what humans already do, but faster.

Among the more nefarious uses of AI by our adversaries are worms that learn how to avoid detection or change behavior on the fly to foil pattern-matching algorithms. An active worm with lateral movement can roam targeted networks undetected for years.

Another risk is intelligent malware that can wait until a set of conditions is met to deploy its payload. And once attackers breach a network, they can use AI to generate activity patterns that confuse intrusion detection systems or overwhelm them with false alerts.

The highly targeted form of the phishing exploit known as "spear phishing" currently requires considerable human effort to create messages that appear to come from known senders. Future algorithms will scrape information from social media accounts and other public sources to create spear phishing messages at scale.

We already do something similar, relying on rough-hewn AI algorithms in sales, to identify potential prospects and distribute messaging around what our algorithms perceive as pain-points.

Sometimes this works OK and sometimes it doesn't. I am frequently reminded of a sales outreach email congratulating a Sales VP on his promotion based on data scraped from an obituary of his predecessor.

While we experiment and fund more start-ups, the use of AI by criminals will potentially bypass – in an instant – entire generations of technical controls that industries have built up over decades.

In the financial services sector, we will soon start to see criminals deploy malware with the ability to capture and exploit voice synthesis technology, mimicking human behavior and biometric data to circumvent authentication of controls for assets found in people's bank accounts, for example.

In short order, the criminal use of AI will generate new attack cycles, highly targeted and deployed for the greatest impact, and in ways that were not thought possible in industries never previously targeted: areas such as biotech, for the theft and manipulation of stored DNA code; mobility, for the hijacking of unmanned vehicles; and healthcare, where ransomware will be timed and deployed for maximum impact.

Biometrics is being widely introduced in different sectors while at the same time raising significant challenges for the global security community. Biometrics and next-generation authentication require high volumes of data about an individual, their activity, and behavior. Voices, faces, and the slightest details of movement and behavioral traits will need to be stored globally, and this will drive cybercriminals to target and exploit a new generation of personal data.

Exploitation will no longer be limited to the theft of people's credit card number but will target the theft of their actual being, their fingerprints, voice identification, and retinal scans.

Most cybersecurity experts agree that three-factor authentication is the best available option, and that two-factor authentication is a baseline must-have. "Know" (password), "have" (token), and "are" (biometrics) are the three factors for authentication, and each one makes this process stronger and more secure. For those CISOs and security analysts charged with defending our assets, understanding an entire ecosystem of biometric software, technology, and storage points makes it even harder to defend the rapidly and ever-expanding attack surface.

This is the "solutionist" ideology at work in the real world.

AI and Biometrics in the near term are not going to solve any of the problems that our current technology stack can't solve. Because most of our breaches and attacks come as the result of poor processes, inadvertent human error, insufficient human resources, and skills, and either too much redundant technologies or too few of the wrong technologies. None of these problems will disappear because we have discovered the world's coolest AI or Biometric solution for cybersecurity defense.

This "solutionist" ideology extends beyond cybersecurity and now influences the discourse around how to handle doctored media.

The solutions being proposed are often technological in nature, from "digital watermarks" to new machine learning forensic techniques. To be sure, there are many experts who are doing important security research to make the detection of fake media and cyber-attacks easier in the future. This is important work and is likely worthwhile. But all by itself, it is unlikely that any AI technology would help prevent cyber-attacks exploiting vulnerabilities that we fail to patch or to fix the deep-seated social problem of truth decay and polarization that social media platforms have played a major role in fostering.

I don't think any technology argument would convince the remaining shareholders of Equifax that an AI solution would have automatically applied the patches necessary to prevent the Apache Struts attack. AI might have generated a loud alert that significant asset values were at risk, but the last time I checked, people still would have had to apply the patch and done the configuration management required to cloak the vulnerability.

System glitches don't occur in a world that runs on the promise of AI or Biometric technology. Banking still runs most of its legacy systems on 220 billion lines of COBOL code, written well before the turn of the century. In 2020, system glitches dominated broad outages triggered by a cyber-attack.

There ain't no magic wands that can automate legacy systems maintenance.

And it is about to get far worse. A new generation of 5G networks will be the single most challenging issue for the cybersecurity landscape. It is not just faster Internet; the design of 5G will mean that the world will enter into an era where, by 2025, 75 billion new devices will be connecting to the Internet every year, running critical applications and infrastructure at nearly 1000 times the speed of the current Internet.

This will provide the architecture for connecting whole new industries, geographies, and communities and at the same time it will hugely alter the threat landscape, as it potentially moves cybercrime from being an invisible, financially driven issue to one where real and serious physical damage will occur at a 5G pace.

5G will provide any attacker with instant access to vulnerable networks. When this is combined with the enterprise and operational technology, a new generation of cyberattacks will emerge, some of which we are already seeing. The ransomware attack against the U.S. city of Baltimore, for example, locked 10,000 employees out of their workstations. In the near future, smart city infrastructures will provide interconnected systems at a new scale, from transport systems for driverless cars, automated water and waste systems, to emergency workers and services, all interdependent, and as highly vulnerable as they are highly connected.

In 2017, the WannaCry attack that took parts of the U.K.'s National Health Service down, required days to spread globally, but in a 5G era, the malware would spread this attack at the speed of light. It is clear that 5G will not only enable great prosperity and help to save people's lives, it will also have the capacity to thrust cybercrime into the real world at a scale and with consequences yet unknown. The bad guys including our nation-state adversaries will be leveraging 5G for maximizing their illicit campaigns, while we will be peddling fast just to stay alive.

We don't have the people or technology to combat and respond to the threats and we don't have the discipline or resources to implement, manage, and maintain the controls necessary to defend our assets.

The most dangerous element evolving from "technological solutionism" is not that industry leaders are coaxed into the chase for the next coolest bright shiny object. It is instead that the ideologyis so easily used as a smokescreen for deep structural problems in the technology industry itself. What is now blindingly obvious to even the most casual observer is that technology alone, had not been able to prevent breaches, loss of data, business interruption, data corruption, and cyber extortion.

In fact, the more technology we develop and apply, and the more money we spend of cybersecurity defense results in a greater increase in cybersecurity breaches. And those breaches are only the ones we (a) know about and (b) are reported. Over the past decade, cyber-criminals have been able to seize on a low-risk, high-reward landscape in which attribution is rare and significant pressure is placed on the traditional levers and responses to cyber-crime.

What I find interesting amid this onslaught is that businesses of all types remain in denial about the threat. It is clear from 10-K filings that still today, despite countless warnings, case studies, and an increase in overall awareness, it is only in the aftermath of a cyber-attack that cybersecurity moves high onto the board agenda in a sustainable way.

In the year before it was hacked, Equifax made just four references to "Cyber, Information Security or Data Security" vs. a credit rating industry average of 17 and an overall U.S. average of 16.

In fact, Equifax's frequency of four matched the average for credit rating agencies way back in 2008, implying a full decade of under-prioritization of security by the company. The term "cyber" is featured more heavily in Equifax's report today than that of leading cyber-security specialist FireEye, who have 117 mentions of "cyber" to Equifax's 139. Equifax's breach costs are currently running to $1.4 billion, while FireEye's entire operating expense equals $1.4 billion over the same period.

Think about that.

Is it obvious that organizations with fewer references to cybersecurity in their annual reporting are less security mature and more likely to be breached? Or, is it more likely that cybersecurity is not high enough on the agenda for the board and executive to feature it in their flagship report?

With the annual report being such a significant communications tool, we can use it as an indicator as to the strength of the top-down security culture within an organization.

But so can our adversaries.

In a stunning example of this information asymmetry, we see that cyber-criminals can follow a similar process as part of their open source intelligence, identifying likely corporate victims perceived as the lowest hanging fruit. It is not a coincidence that Marriot, Anthem, Equifax, Yahoo, Home Depot, Sony, Adobe, etc., were among the many with the fewest references to cybersecurity in their pre-breach 10'Ks.

If we stay in denial and do nothing to change the course, in the next few years, the cybersecurity landscape will worsen significantly and any chance of protecting information assets, assuring truthful social media, and providing data privacy will disappear completely.

Existential threats? Forget about Global Warming. Years from now, we all may all be speaking a different language.

How can we reverse course and get ahead?

1. First, change the reporting rules and prevent companies from reporting on their cyber-vulnerabilities;

2. Second, close down all Chinese-owned venture capital firms;

3. Third, stop buying hardware made in China;

4. Fourth, stop using any products or services, including mobile devise and telecom made in China;

5. Fifth, start sharing in earnest between public and private sectors;

6. Sixth, modernize our cyber-laws to enable offensive security;

7. Seventh, mandate a Zero Trust architecture and migration for every network within an aggressive time-frame,

8. Eighth, create and enforce national security mandates that specify technologies that must be part of every Zero Trust implementation,

9. Ninth, create the equivalent of a Manhattan project for the application of AI/ML to the problem space, with appropriate funding and speed to market; and

10. Tenth, implement mandates on insurance providers to match coverage against a standardized NIST framework requirement. Let

them figure out the Towers - they know how and managed to do so with AIG.

By removing excessive trust from our systems and networks, isolating our critical assets, amping the identity authentication process, and reducing the overall attack surface, we will have removed 50% of the breach risk, and made cyber-criminals jobs much harder.

By eliminating products and services provided by our number one adversary, we will put an end to pre-engineered leakage and impossible to detect hardware vulnerabilities.

By throwing the IP thieves out of our tents, we will stop the theft of the key technologies that our adversaries now use against us.

By modernizing cybersecurity laws, we will remove the handcuffs that currently hinder law enforcement from apprehension and prosecution. In addition, we can open the doorways to a controlled offensive or forward defensive cybersecurity program at the national level, so that targets and victims can identify and seize bad actors in the process of committing their crimes.

By establishing mandates (vs. recommended) national security rules, we will assure that every organization is building and managing their IT and OT systems in accord with best practices that have demonstrated their ability to increase resiliency while decreasing risk. One mandate can cover Ransomware attacks, by preventing the payout, but also providing insured coverage for the damage recovery, adjusting for negligence and attendant liability, within a year of the attack under the jurisdiction of a special court.

By insisting on a mutual sharing of information and intelligence, private industry will have access to signals and behavioral data, now protected which will enrich new product design and development.

By an instituting an aggressive AI/ML Manhattan project, we will be able to expand the concept of a YCombinator with a specific product focus, aggressive funding, curation, and vetting and guidance from experts in those disciplines. It took only four years and $2 billion ($40 billion in 2022 dollars) to produce FatMan from whole cloth – it should take half that time and twice the money today.

By forcing insurers to provide and align their coverage against a standard for proper defense and controls, the burden is transferred to NAIC and FIO, forcing an actuarial proxy that will mature over time, yet set consistent expectations for both insurers and insured.

If we do all of this, will cyber-crime come to an end? Will we reverse the asymmetry within our current attacker/defender dynamic? Will we achieve world peace?

Of course not, BUT … .

It will begin a reversal of course and shift momentum to our team.

World War II history revives similarities between then and now, and underscores the possibility, and in fact, the outright probability, of success in re-engineering that asymmetry and creating an even playing field.

Professor Richard Overy, the famed British historian reminds us, that while in his prison cell at Nuremberg, Hitler's foreign minister, Joachim von Ribbentrop, wrote a brief memoir in the course of which he explored the reasons for Germany's defeat. He picked out three factors that he thought were critical: the unexpected "power of resistance" of the Red Army; the vast supply of American armaments; and the success of Allied air power.

British forces were close to defeat everywhere in 1942. The American economy was a peacetime economy, apparently unprepared for the colossal demands of total war. The Soviet system was all but shattered in 1941, two-thirds of its heavy industrial capacity captured, and its vast air and tank armies destroyed. This was a war, Ribbentrop ruefully concluded, that "Germany could have won."

Soviet resistance was in some ways the most surprising outcome. The German attackers believed that Soviet Communism was a corrupt and primitive system that would collapse, in Goebbels' words "like a pack of cards."

The evidence of how poorly the Red Army fought in 1941 confirmed these expectations. More than five million Soviet soldiers were captured or killed in six months; they fought with astonishing bravery, but at every level of combat were out-classed by troops that were better armed, better trained and better led.

This situation seemed beyond remedy.

Yet within a year, Soviet factories were out-producing their richly endowed German counterparts – the Red Army had embarked on a thorough transformation of the technical and organizational base of Soviet forces, and a stiffening of morale, from Stalin downward, produced the first serious reverse for the German armed forces when Operation Uranus in November 1942 led to the encirclement of Stalingrad and the loss of the German Sixth Army.

Within a year.

The Russian air and tank armies were reorganized to mimic the German Panzer divisions and air fleets; communication and intelligence were vastly improved (helped by a huge supply of American and British telephone equipment and cable); training for officers and men was designed to encourage greater initiative; and the technology available was hastily modernized to match Germany's.

The ability of the world's largest industrial economy to convert to the mass production of weapons and war equipment is usually taken for granted. Yet the transition from peace to war was so rapid and effective that America was able to make up for the lag in building up effectively trained armed forces by exerting a massive material production superiority.

This success owed something to the experience of Roosevelt's New Deal, when for the first time, the federal government began to operate its own economic planning agencies; and it owed something to the decision by the American armed forces in the 1920s to focus on issues of production and logistics in the Industrial War College set up in Washington.

But above all it owed a great deal to the character of American industrial capitalism, with its "can-do" ethos, high levels of engineering skill, and tough-minded entrepreneurs. After a decade of recession, the manufacturing community had a good deal of spare, unemployed capacity to absorb (unlike Germany, where full employment was reached well before the outbreak of war, and gains in output could only really come from improvements in productivity).

Even with these vast resources at hand, however, it took American forces considerable time before they could fight on equal terms with well-trained and determined enemies.

This gap in fighting effectiveness helps to explain the decision taken in Washington to focus a good deal of the American effort on the building up of a massive air power. Roosevelt saw air strategy as a key to future war and a way to reduce American casualties.

At his encouragement, the Army Air Forces were able to build up an air force that came to dwarf those of Germany and Japan. At the center of the strategy was a commitment to strategic bombing, the long-range and independent assault on the economic and military infrastructure.

Bombing provided the key difference between the western Allies and Germany. It played an important part in sustaining domestic morale in Britain and the USA, while its effects on German society produced social disruption on a vast scale (by late 1944, 8 million Germans had fled from the cities to the safer villages and townships).

The debilitating effects on German air power then reduced the contribution German aircraft could make on the Eastern Front, where Soviet air forces vastly outnumbered German. The success of air power in Europe persuaded the American military leaders to try to end the war with Japan the same way.

City raids from May 1945 destroyed a vast area of urban Japan and paved the way for a surrender, completed with the dropping of the two atomic bombs in August 1945. Here, too, the American government and public were keen to avoid further heavy casualties.

Difficult decisions then; impossible decisions now.

There were weaknesses and strengths in Hitler's strategy, but no misjudgments were more costly in the end than the German belief that the Red Army was a primitive force, incapable of prolonged resistance, or Hitler's insistence that America would take years to rearm and could never field an effective army, or the failure to recognize that bombing was a threat worth taking seriously before it was too late.

Military arrogance and political hubris put Germany on the path to a war she could have won only if these expectations had proved true.

There are lots of moving parts, economic, tribal, social, political, geophysical, psychological, and logistical that fall into the stew of wartime decisions. But they all do.

There are so many similarities in our current story when compared with our wartime history dating back only 70 years, we would be foolish to ignore them. Learning from history, however cumbersome, rather than repeating every step, is always a good strategy for survival.

It is now critically important for every American citizen to review its WW Two history against the current backdrop of this existential, cybersecurity threat; this undeclared declaration of war; this real and present danger to our lifestyles, freedom, beliefs, ideology, social, and cultural fabric and our entire future way of life.

There is still time, and given that we can accept what must be done, steps, and processes like we've described will pave the way for action, but only if we are all committed to change.

Changing the world has been a sink-hole of human energy for hundreds of years – changing ourselves is much harder to do, because it starts with admitting we have been in denial, but not unlike other habits, one step leads to another.

Professor Richard Overy's brilliant historical novel, "World War Two: How the Allies Won" is a great place to start.

INFORMATION

As we crossed the border at Quartzite, we realized suddenly that the information we had was wrong. We were headed into Arizona but we had no idea how to get there.

Information? What do we mean exactly?

In the context of cybersecurity, we are not talking about information warfare per-se, or even intelligence about threats, though it plays a factor. What is typically meant by information in our context, conjures up the recent Russian meddling and Asian psycho-warfare, and is certainly not new. Threat intelligence has been around a while as well, though there have been some recent advances which are interesting and may be useful to help us get to know our adversaries better.

To be precise, the Information Theater to which we are referring relates to one of the core elements of the attacker–defender dynamic where our attackers know lots of stuff about us, while we know very little and in many cases, nothing about them. This, of course, provides a tremendous battlefield advantage to the other team. This asymmetric element sets our very siloed and segmented defenses up against masquerading attackers about whom we have almost no information, and they consequently require very little of their own to be successful.

Informational asymmetry also results in our continuing failure to identify the exploitation of legitimacy (fakery) or ability to correctly attribute the source or nature of our attackers.

We are never sure whether Russia or Iran or China or young Robert Francis Baker living in his mom's basement down on First Street is the actual attacker. And it dramatically affects our ability to respond to or even develop a policy for response protocols.

As one of many examples, it appears that China likely recruited the hacker who pulled off the massive cyberattack on Anthem where 78.8 million consumer records were exposed ... but we don't know that for sure. Even though seven state insurance commissioners conducted a nationwide examination of the breach over a three-year period and in addition, hired Mandiant to run its own internal investigation, we still don't know.

For sure.

In spite of uncovering only the apparent source IP address, this army of investigators concluded that the hack originated in China and began when a user at an Anthem subsidiary opened a phishing email which gave the hacker access to Anthem's data warehouse.

The hack was of course devastating to Anthem and the 80 million covered who lost all of their sensitive PII, but while we now know how it was carried out, we are unable to conclusively determine the actual perpetrator.

The result of all of this investigation and the more than $300 million Anthem has spent in recovery and forensics is a slight increase in general awareness about the nature of our adversaries, but a widening of the actual information gap itself. We think it was China and we "know" they are always doing this sort of thing, but that information does not advance our ability to defend in the future.

We don't know who we are fighting, unless the U.S. government agencies does, and they aren't telling.

This information gap contributes to another imbalance in attacker–defender dynamics where we stack up a relatively small contingent of trained defenders protecting millions of applications and systems located in fixed positions against tens of thousands of unknown global cyber attackers continuously examining tens of millions of dispersed targets.

In terms of military tactics, state armies like ours generally fight in an orderly framework while non-state and individual terrorist organizations successfully use guerrilla warfare methods designed to leverage the disparities in power advantage.

Since we don't know who we are fighting and we must defend fixed positions without specific rules of engagement, it makes it difficult to successfully engage and almost impossible to imagine victory.

Our adversaries regularly probe and collect reams of information about our cybersecurity defenses. This is not difficult to do since we openly publish all of our academic cybersecurity research and in the few cases where we don't publish, our adversaries just steal our IP anyway.

Reverse engineering an AI/ML cyber defense system to discover the methods it uses to provide that defense is not hard to do. Which systems deploy which technologies is easy too. U.S. product vendors proudly broadcast the sources and at a macro level, and even the techniques.

A classic example can be found in Security Information and Event Management (SIEM) systems.

Love them or dismiss their effectiveness, a SIEM is a widely acknowledged cybersecurity fundamental requirement for monitoring, detecting, and alerting in near-real-time the presence of malware or a threat vector present in our computing infrastructure.

Though there are other approaches like network behavioral monitors, all enterprises must have some way to determine the presence of a threat and to notify early respondents so they can move to mitigate before the damage spreads.

The Achilles with SIEMs and with all other behavioral detection systems is the detection threshold. Those thresholds (aka policies) for the detection of certain behaviors must be set low enough so that a brute force password attack (for example) cannot evade the detection but not so low that activity other than brute force attacks triggers an alert and results in a false positive.

Set too low, the system will generate tons of false positives. Set too high, and the system will fail to catch true predators. These threshold variations are not secrets.

SIEM and network monitoring vendors publish the default ranges along with recommended settings. Since IT resources are under continual pressure, the natural response is to accept the defaults and install as recommended. This enables even the most dim-witted attacker to tune the vulnerability probe to fly beneath the radar and look for software holes, open backdoors, available credentials, and other keys to the kingdom. Those findings are reported back to the C&C and this data informs the next cyber-attack on that enterprise.

We don't know what we don't know.

These low and slow vulnerability probes go on for months and years, collecting and distributing useful information back to the attackers. Probes are likely floating around your network infrastructure as you read this. By having less information than our attackers, we unintentionally provide a fully cooperative pathway to the next series of breaches.

Less is not more.

Attackers frequently scan many thousands of potential targets before a successful compromise, and much is learned from each one. We have an abundance of online hacker communities willingly dispensing reams of information, how-to tutorials for every kind of hack imaginable, instructions in the use of available open-source penetration testing tools, and malware kits tailored by attack type with complete user manuals that describe in detail the steps required to deploy.

The defenders have information security communities like ISACA and ISC2, industry conferences like RSA, and vendor product user groups, but our ability to connect information to execution does not compare to the way the bad guys do it.

Big hat, no cattle.

In other words, we talk a lot about this stuff, but we do very little in terms of actually implementing best practices.

Our adversaries are busy deploying their well-informed attack protocols while our information security community is continually distracted by the necessities of daily survival.

Back when we first advanced this thesis in 2015, an ideologically driven actor (who was known as HackBack!) was running rampant with a slew of significant cyber-attacks including a big one against the Italian surveillance technology company "Hacking Team."

Motivated by what he perceived to be human-rights concerns, Mr. HackBack!, managed to compromise their internal network and publicly release 400 GB of data which included email correspondence between employees at the company and their clients, proprietary source code, financial records, sensitive audio, and video files.

Then he published a set of instructions detailing exactly how he mounts his attacks including the schematic for a zero-day exploit that he had developed himself.

He followed that with a published a list of off-the-shelf tools and specific guidance on using exploit kits to carry out similar compromises. After the hijacked data was made publicly available via Twitter, and a fully searchable database was hosted on WikiLeaks, the company suffered significant and embarrassing reputational damage and had a global operational license revoked.

In just a few days after the breach, two exploit kits, Angler and Neutrino, which have now morphed into far more advanced EKs, had incorporated new exploits revealed in Mr. HackBack!'s publications, increasing their functionality and assisting other cybercriminals to compromise new targets with new malware.

In response to the growing imbalance, the federal government began encouraging businesses to share threat intelligence among themselves, but almost every business has ignored the suggestion. We keep trying to address the issue in forums, seminars and conferences instead.

There is sort of a weird layer of general apathy that hangs around the surface of this industry, where it feels constantly like a streak of existential acquiescence, as in … "there's really nothing we can do but let's keep pushing this boulder up the mountain anyway."

Recently, the Cyber Security and Infrastructure Security Agency (CISA) launched the Joint Cyber Defense Collaborative (JCDC), which is a joint collaboration between federal agencies and the private sector led by CISA the to strengthen the nation's cyber defenses through planning, preparation, and information sharing. The purpose of the JCDC, is to establish an "office for joint cyber planning" to develop "for public and private entities" plans to defend against cyber-attacks posing a risk to critical infrastructure or national interests.

Congress was acting on one of the Cyber Space Solarium Commission's recommendations, which noted in its report that the sheer number of U.S. cyber security agencies makes it difficult "to achieve the unity of effort required to conduct layered cyber defense" as well as to "collaborate with the private sector and conduct cyber operations as part of whole-of-nation campaigns."

And whole of nation campaigns are what we need.

Those of us in the private sector have all agreed that the plethora of various public-private partnerships led by different federal agencies, was at best, confusing. The JCDC aims to correct for that, creating a unified effort among government agencies and private sector partners to share threat information, validate it, and act upon it.

The idea is to be proactive, not reactive, so when an attack does occur both public and private sector entities will know who will be responsible for certain actions, and how to respond. We shouldn't be trying to figure things out after every attack. What feels different with the JCDC is that both the public and private sector will be planning our responses together. Multiple agencies and multiple companies will be offering their insight on how to best defend our nation against cyber-attacks. While the initial focus will be on ransomware attacks and securing the cloud, other defenses should be readied as the threat landscape evolves.

As National Cyber Director Chris Inglis stated, if the JCDC works as imagined, the "adversary will need to beat all of us to beat one of us."

On another promising front, we have recently made some progress in threat intelligence technologies that may have a small but favorable impact. Threat intelligence is actually a potentially useful way to start shifting some of the imbalance by providing insight into what the bad guys are doing and prompting companies to rebalance their cybersecurity defense portfolio accordingly.

It is one of the very few approaches that has a chance of actually providing a little immediate information relief as it offers current insights about emerging threats and their evolution.

These systems track adversaries across multiple types of unique and hard-to-reach online communities, from elite forums and illicit marketplaces to chat services platforms, and then they provide visibility into cybercrime and fraud practices, international, political, and societal dynamics, trends with malware and exploits, specifics about disruption and destructive threats, and physical and insider activities.

By providing an intelligence profile of the threat landscape, this contextual view offers concrete input to enable enterprises to more effectively rebalance their cyber-defense portfolios with respect to emerging and existing threats, adversaries, and relevant business risks.

This is of course a whole lot different than having Mr. HackBack!'s instruction manual and $50 for an exploit kit. But at least defenders now have some information about the adversarial community and may be able to determine effective cybersecurity technologies and processes to which it can shift the emphasis and stave off a few of these attack vectors. It costs a lot of money, takes a lot of resources, needs support at the executive level, and is not easy to implement.

It's something, but alone, it is nowhere near enough.

Knowing more about our adversaries and their behavior is about to become even more critical as we embark into the IoT world in earnest. A simple example of how IoT threats pose significantly higher risk can be found in the recent graduation of the Mirai botnet into a grander version of itself. This new descendant is casting a much wider net than its predecessors and is now infecting systems normally found outside of traditional IT enterprises.

The entire world of industrial control systems and SCADA are highly vulnerable, based solely on the fact that the devices themselves are old, have little to no built in security, control 99% of our critical infrastructure across all segments (energy, water, food, transportation, communication, and military), and almost no IoT devices can be either updated or secured from being drawn into a botnet army, or addressed from a pure Cybersecurity defense point of view.

One can shut down an ERP system for days to patch and apply security updates, but try that with an automotive plant sometime.

One other point of light is on the back end, where cybercriminals use crypto exchanges to launder cryptocurrency into fiat currency through a myriad and complex network of mixed crypto content and multiple digital wallets.

Companies like TRM Labs who are using blockchain to trace the source and destination of cryptocurrency transactions, compile risk profiles for wallets, addresses and entities, including high-risk on-chain activity or affiliates, and trace the flow of funds across many different blockchains and hundreds of thousands of assets.

The more mature the industry gets, the more blockchains and assets will become available. Forensics like these are vital to the FBI and DOJ in the disruption, apprehension, and prosecution of cyber-criminals following a successful attack.

Yet, for all these steps in the right direction, we have seen the attacker/defender dynamic in Information growing in complexity and has broadly expanded the gap that has developed over the last few years.

So what can we do to address this gap?

1. Begin with a re-architecture of our systems, networks, applications, and access – this is not as daunting as it appears – by localized protect surfaces surrounding key assets, we isolate them from the rest of the network and attack surface landscape, forcing our adversaries to reveal more about themselves or abandon their journey altogether.

2. Centralize and distribute threat intelligence in an efficient, actionable format which feeds into and expands our visibility into threat actors and their behaviors.

3. Openly and jointly share the vulnerability data that we now hoard privately, so that both private and public get boosted insight into collateral threats and can deal with them more effectively than flying blind, hoping for a random kill.

4. Modernize our current laws to enable both private and public entities together and separately to mount offensives against the known, documented and evidence traced markets, forums, and illicit distribution centers on the dark web.

5. Adopt a more aggressive cybersecurity posture so we can be more efficiently monitoring adversaries in real-time in order to understand what they are doing and planning to do and who they are.

At the end of the day, we also need a galvanizing central force who can force us all to end this cowboy approach to cybersecurity defense that has led only to increased cyber-crime and more breaches.

We all love our horses, and are loath to dismount, but the time has come to join a larger movement that can form a united front and attack the battlefield asymmetry across all five theaters of war.

Until these steps are taken, it appears that the information gap will continue to expand, and the farther it does, the more difficult it will be to bridge with new suspension technologies, and it will keep us sliding backwards enabling our enemies to advance.

History is a good teacher, but only if we pay attention, and act.

ECONOMICS

The years flew by and as I assessed my net worth, I was dismayed to find that I was now capable of living the life that Thoreau had suggested, yet I was presently incapable of transcendentalism in any form. It occurred to me that money is not the answer to all questions.

A few years ago, circa 2015, we offered the notion of the existence of four separate theaters of cyber-warfare. If you broke it all down, we were faced with asymmetric attacker/defender dynamics in five theaters: Economics, Information, Education, Leadership, and Technology.

The principal argument of our thesis was that we were being out-gunned, outpaced, and outdistanced in each theater and when combined, we were fighting an adversarial enemy of overwhelming strength.

The argument back then couldn't be more accurate than when applied to today's environment.

Economic considerations continue to widen the gap between our ability to defend against cyberattacks and our adversary's ability to launch them. We've seen the following economic trends:

Increasing cyber investment decisions at the board level.

Expansive digitization initiatives.

Securing legacy systems and expanding technical debt.

Market demand for complex cybersecurity technologies.

We operate in a world where some "random dude" with a laptop, an internet connection and $25 can attack JP Morgan Chase bank (which is spending over a half billion dollars a year on cybersecurity defense).

And the "random dude" often wins.

Worldwide spending on cybersecurity is predicted to top $1 trillion for the five-year period from 2017 to 2021. In early 2017, Lloyd's of London claimed that cybercrime was costing businesses globally up to $600 billion a year. But the whisper number is more like $1.5 trillion.

To contrast this, if we bought every exploit kit available on the dark web, we would be hard-pressed to spend $100,000. If we went instead to the Russian, German, Chinese, Brazilian, Japanese, and Canadian underground markets, we might add another $100,000.

The Dark Web Candy Store includes the following attack vectors, processes, disguises, and ruses:

ATM PIN pad skimmers and bots,

Credit card clones

Credit card number generators and Crypters

Exploit Kits

Fake websites

How-to guides/modules

Malware itself or Malware-as-a-Service

Social engineering toolkits,

And to bring it all into a monetary perspective, anyone with $50 can purchase a perfectly good and in excellent working order Distributed Denial-of-service (DDoS) attack. The flavors are plentiful: floods, pings of death, fragmented packets, low-and-slows or zero- days, etc.

According to the Behind the Dark Net Black Mirror report published in 2021, the last three years has seen a 20% rise in the number of dark web listings targeting the enterprise.

Malware and DDoS kits now represent almost half of the attack kits for sale. The highly rated Nuke malware is being heavily marketed because of its uniquely destructive signature.

Not only does it allow users to open remote sessions and effectively take over an infected machine, it easily bypasses most flavors of Windows firewall protections used by the typical enterprise customer. You can find many discussion threads in Russian- language forums actively applauding Nuke as the ideal attack tool for use against enterprise networks.

While all sectors are targeted by hackers, banking, and finance were the most popular (based on Willie Sutton's law), followed by e-commerce, healthcare, education and media platforms. Over 60% of sellers are offering access to more than ten business networks and in many cases, the credentials are priced as low as $2 each. These are a cheap entry into the world of cybercrime, effective, and readily available to novice hackers who can't spend a lot of time learning how to use the tools.

This same study found that just under half of dark web sellers were offering services that specifically target FTSE 100 or Fortune 500 companies, and depending on the company involved, these services could be purchased for as little as $150.

Even the most expensive service is only $10,000, a mere rounding error against the $12 Billion Jamie Dimon spent in 2021to defend against these exact same threat vectors at JP Morgan Chase. Yes. Less than one tiny fraction of 1% of Chase Bank's entire Cybersecurity budget in 2021 gets you the most expensive enterprise cyber-attack kit on the entire underground market. The economic imbalance is breathtaking.

The accumulating data makes it seem like we are operating as a fourth world country trying to compete with global economic powers. While the reverse is obviously true, you wouldn't know it by assessing the results. The fact is that we are watching it happen, we report on it daily now, and we don't seem to be able to know what to do or how to contain it. By continuing to expand our threat landscape, we not only encourage its growth, but we are actually building the very highway the attackers are using.

In the past 20 years, the nature of corporate asset value has changed significantly. More than 85% of the value of Fortune 500 companies consists today of intellectual property (IP) and other intangibles. With this rapidly expanding digitization of assets comes a corresponding digitization of corporate risk.

Corporations worldwide are losing hundreds of billions of dollars annually from the loss of IP, trading algorithms, destroyed or altered financial and consumer data, diminished reputations, and heightened risk exposure through increased regulatory and legal liabilities.

The risk increases with each newly passed regulation and data privacy law.

Constant internal pressure to leverage new paths to digitization, exploding attack vectors, and the shift in both professional and now personal liability for C-level executives and Board members creates additional layers of economic risk unprecedented in the history of business.

Legacy enterprise systems which remain the backbone of most corporate operations were designed without any security in mind and are becoming even more insecure.

Wells Fargo and most major banks still rely on ancient Check Processing and Customer Management systems that were developed well before the turn of the century and the life of those systems is being extended through new technologies designed for exactly that purpose.

Instead of ripping and replacing, most companies are opting for legacy life-line extension, hoping to get even more mileage out of these old enterprise systems as a whole category of new software companies offering front-ends or analytic tools requiring only large lakes of data have emerged to pump new oxygen and even more layers onto these ancient piles of code.

Multiple studies including the Escaping Legacy report by Accenture have found that 50% of all banking IT assets are in critical need of modernization and an incredible 43% of all banking systems are still running on 220 billion lines of COBOL code.

The resistance to change is enormous as the economics to do so are prohibitive.

In addition to the availability of new life extenders, we have repeatedly patched these systems throughout the years, layering newer technologies over old ones, and rendering them almost impossible for new software engineers to deconstruct decades' worth of complex workarounds.

Today's COBOL programmers are in their 70's, so the future doesn't look real bright.

Delaying the inevitable creates enormous technical debt. When companies take shortcuts, over time these quick fixes accumulate and almost always manifest into system failures and vulnerabilities that hackers can easily exploit.

To further exacerbate the risk, cloud computing is seen as an economically desirable alternative to native hosting, and these applications are increasingly used in a hybrid role where they can be connected to older systems that are then treated as reliable plumbing.

The downside to this strategy is that we increase system vulnerabilities by placing critical assets in what are fundamentally insecure cloud environments.

Companies like Microsoft, Yahoo, Apple, DropBox, and LinkedIn have all suffered cloud security breaches. Cloud computing relies entirely upon the Internet and by definition is difficult to secure. While there are many ways to mitigate these threats, the IT community, for a variety of reasons has proven that we are not very good at it and the effect of moving data and computing to the cloud is an expanded threat landscape.

Yet, JPMorgan Chase for one, is doubling down on this strategy and plans on "refactoring" most of its applications in the coming months to the cloud. While the economic attacker/defender dynamic, as played out in corporate boardrooms and within IT organizations works increasingly in favor of attackers, the corollary technologies used for attack are cheaper than they ever have been.

While it is always very difficult to present an ROI on cyber-attacks that have been prevented, we are also not very good when it comes to communicating with decision makers about risk.

Since we cannot, or choose not, to quantify risk in terms that C-level executives can understand, we are always asking for budget increases based on expressing risk in terms of "high" or "very high" instead of $ millions or billions.

This resistance to fund necessary tools and human resources shouldn't be surprising.

Since we are unable to defend our thesis about the risks we are trying to mitigate in quantitative arguments with decision makers who speak and think in economic terms, we should not be surprised when our requests are denied.

The economic pressures on the growth side are compelling, yet they create difficult Cybersecurity management challenges and massively increased complexity:

1. The push to embrace technologies like cloud computing without proper controls,

2. The expansion of connectivity driving uncontrolled and networked IoT,

3. An enthusiasm for broad BYOD and BYOC programs,

4. The digitization of everything,

5. An increased reliance upon third parties for provision and supply-chain components,

6. Our refusal to replace and our insistence upon extending our dangerous legacy systems,

7. The enormous supply and demand gap for competent information security resources,

8. Our negligence with proper hygiene, training, education, and process,

9. Our inability to shift our strategy to offensively managing risk vs. defensively managing cybersecurity,

These challenges are driven largely by economic considerations and combine to expand the gap between our ability to defend and our attackers' capacity to strike.

The rational conclusion is that the economic dynamics have grown more complex and have worsened the outlook.

If we continue with this narrow historical approach to cybersecurity defense, it is likely that we will compound the problem space even further.

What looks like a widening gap today could well become an impossible chasm tomorrow.

The way out requires a slight pumping of brakes. And this is where once again, Zero Trust comes to the rescue.

A Zero Trust strategy can work around all of the impediments we've just described to identify and isolate our critical assets, segment them within manageable protect surfaces protected by granular controls at the level 7 application layer, require MFA for initial access, and continuously monitor session behavior requiring repetitive MFA for subsequent requests as well.

We reduce the attack surface, extinguish excessive trust throughout the network, increase rigor and discipline in identity access management, are able to quantify the value of the assets we are protecting, lessen complexity and make the cyber-criminals' work harder.

All of this results in fewer successful attacks and an ability to explain to our C-suite and Boards of Directors exactly how we are accomplishing this in language they can understand.

LEADERSHIP

Sam called and left a message. It said he didn't know how to get to Farley's. I knew, sort of, but who am I to lead anyone anywhere? I locked the doors, left a treat for the cat and went to bed.

From all appearances, leadership is missing in action.

Given my background, I empathize with cybersecurity leadership and can't imagine trying to do the job at current expectation levels during the storm in which we find ourselves. The competition between business unit owners driving toward the fourth industrial revolution, pockets of shadow IT running unknown quantities of cloud sessions, increased dependencies on supply-chains, open-source everywhere, new heights of network complexity, a lack of available resources to fill the gaps, and increased sophistication and smarter attacks from cybercriminals along with promises of safely and security from 3500 point solution vendors would drive anyone crazy.

If you have a CISO who appears to be keeping the lights on, make sure they are happy.

For every competent CISO, there must be a dozen who aren't.

But CISO leadership is not limited to technology choices, maturity programs, operations and governance, and the provisioning of adequate detection and protection capabilities to assure a computing environment is safe from bad guys.

It is responsible to the company and shareholders to do everything possible to assure maximum protection and the implementation and support of well-thought out and carefully designed layers of defense, leveraging the best and most effective technology tools, the optimal use of available resources, the appropriate levels of education and training delivered to the right people at the right time, and communication with C-suite and Board members at a level where both sides can operate from the same page of the play book, at all times.

In addition, in most corporate IT environments, the relationships between the IT leaders and the security leaders appear opposed or operate with a substantial amount of friction. One requires the absolute cooperation with the other to enable their programs and achieve their goals, cooperation that is not always forthcoming.

The relationship between the board, C-suite, and the CISO is often ill-suited to the execution of actionable programs as the definitions of accountability and responsibility are soft-peddled and generally ignored by the senior party.

This translates to responsibility and even accountability on paper but not extended in fact or downright withheld in practice, leading to mistrust and an inordinate amount of anti-productive meetings, analysis, and proposals.

My experience is that the board simply does not trust either the IT or Security leadership; they don't trust that either team understands the business nor could make the right executive decisions were they in charge, and as a consequence, the board will not relinquish the reins of leadership outside of their domains. The CISO doesn't seem to be able to grasp business basics or understand for example the notion of risk transfer.

We hear frequently that 99% of the global business leaders claim cyber risk is the greatest risk facing our economy and when Fed Chairman Jerome Powell said on 60 Minutes that the greatest risk to the economy is cyber risk, we assume that our business leaders are all on the same page.

They don't worry about inflation, another financial crisis or another a pandemic—they worry about cyber risk.

The World Economic Forum (WEF) Global Risk Report 2021, tells us that the top three short-term risks to the world, as defined by its survey of 650 WEF leaders, are infectious disease, income inequality, and extreme weather events. The fourth, is cybersecurity. Nearly 40% of WEF leaders cited cybersecurity as a "clear and present danger" to the global economy.

While we have seen some degree of global cooperation around the first three issues, we have not seen that same level of cooperation around cybersecurity. The Convention on Cybercrime (AKA the Budapest Convention) has been ratified by 65 nations, but focuses primarily on nation states assisting each other in the prosecution of cybercrimes, not addressing today's nation states attacking private sector companies at will.

Are 65 companies asleep at the wheel or have they all signed up for Chinese protection under the BRI initiative?

Even though we have seen these attacks in action now for years, we still have no Convention-like treaty that establishes rules of engagement for nation states in cyberspace and provides a legal framework for the international prosecution of violators.

And as a consequence, nothing will change the global landscape for private or public leadership with regard to cyber-crime and cyber-attacks. Without modernized laws at a whole of global government level, it is impossible to impress upon the decision makers in private companies to break from the pack.

Risk transfer will remain the Sleepeze for board members unless and until our CISO leadership community determines that it is their responsibility to force reality into their presentations in a way that the board can both grok and understand the details of liability as they relate to their fiduciary responsibilities.

Until then, business as usual.

As a result, without changing the way that CISO's manage within their organizations, the lack of leadership will always be one of the great Achilles' heels of the Cybersecurity space. It is the equivalent of laws that protect retail criminals form prosecution if all they steal is valued below $900.

As even casual observers will recall, it only took Colonial one day to decide on a $5 million ransomware payment, in spite of aggressive Federal and Law Enforcement advice to the contrary.

That is risk transfer in action and it did nothing to help prevent another attack, either to Colonial or its brethren's pipeline companies worldwide.

What we need is for the CISO to step into the breach – to embrace a true leadership role – which translates to defining a path forward that will minimize the probability of a catastrophic event.

This means having the courage to architect and promote an enterprise-wide Zero Trust strategy that begins with third-party assessment, a rigorous identification of critical assets, an isolation of these assets through micro-segmentation and access protection through granular identity management and policy engines with a fully saturated monitoring of lateral activity beyond initial entry through to behavior while on the networks and upon session exits, the dedication of fully staffed cybersecurity hygiene programs, and the discipline to adhere to best practices throughout.

It means translating that strategy into language that the board will understand and contextualized outside the standard threat/consequence matrix, so that professional risk decision makers can make determinations aligned with realities that they can now understand.

We may not be able to fix leadership issues at the national or international levels, but nothing stops us from doing so within our own domains.

Other than fear.

CHAPTER 3

The Impact of the Last 20 Years

The drums beat loudly, but from our position atop the castle parapets, we could only hear the faintest echoes of patterned hammering as if the heavens were whispering of distant danger approaching.

The whole compound was built by artisans who traveled here from throughout the territories. Electricians and plumbers. Carpenters and concrete crews. As I walk through the remains, I notice that the locks are still intact. Doors still standing in doorframes, as impenetrable as the day they were installed 40 years ago.

As we review our most recent breach activity, we see a pattern emerging which is a departure from the historic norm, and one which likely portends a difficult future state.

It is a state with which we are unprepared to assimilate, due to the "protect and defend" architectural design of our cyber-defense technologies, combined with our constitutional guardrails and our confirmation biases toward our adversaries.

To wit, 99+% of our software tools are not engineered to detect or discover threat vectors like those used in the SolarWinds, Accellion, and Microsoft attacks and our rule of law, which currently prevents the execution of offensive techniques and tactics outside our networks. We are also inclined to believe that cybercriminals are seeking immediate financial rewards (ransomware) or the extraction of data which, when

DOI: 10.1201/9781003331773-4

combined with other data, creates assets of value that can be sold on the dark web for delayed financial benefit.

While both of those things are true, it is also true that something deeply sinister is operating either in parallel or in place of those motivations. A course that is focused on intelligence gathering and channels of disruption, animated through cyber-ops dis-mis-mal-information distribution and dissemination, and having little or nothing to do with financial gains.

It is clear that the SolarWinds attack was a nation-state attack intent upon, and succeeding in, the disruption of our entire Federal network infrastructure and resulting in the panicked response that followed.

Both Russia and China have shifted their positioning toward us in the ensuing weeks, with messaging that clearly conveys the sentiment that they no longer live in fear of their western adversary who has now been exposed to enjoy the latest version of the emperors' clothing line.

Some in the media argue that this advance in acrimony results from the current administration's history of projecting weakness toward these two giants, which may in some part contribute, but I suspect instead that with the recent experiments in supply chain exploitation, both adversaries feel comfortably confident in their cyber-superiority.

The future for the invaders seems bright, as Kevin Mandia, the CEO of FireEye, pointed out during his congressional testimony that "Modifying the software build process, rather than the source code, means that this is a more portable attack and will show up in more places than just SolarWinds."

The key questions on the SolarWinds attack swirled around why so many public and private entities failed for months to detect the hack, and why did only one of the tens of thousands of victims eventually find it?

After combing through tons of threat intelligence and forensics evidence, FireEye discovered the hack after it became a "stage-two" victim. Stage one entailed the bad guys compromising SolarWinds Inc. and its Orion software by the ghostly insertion of a backdoor into a software update. Stage two casualties are anyone who downloaded the legitimate, yet compromised, update that was infected during stage one.

Mandia also told congress that he believed the attack required a multiyear preparation journey and Microsoft President Brad Smith, testifying in the same hearing, said the hack involved the work of "at least 1,000 engineers." While perhaps self-serving, these observations underscore a time frame and resourcing that are hugely impressive, almost as breathtaking as the fact that we failed to detect any of it while it was going on right under our noses.

MISSION REVEAL

General (Ret.) Keith Alexander, the CEO of IronNet observed: "I think the real objective is to gain information; they want insights into what's going on in our country. There have been no insights yet as to the Russians actually setting landmines as opposed to gathering information, but we can think of this as the recon phase. During this point of intrusion, they could set up backdoors so they have a way of getting in and out of the networks."

> You don't necessarily have to set up landmines at that time; you would probably keep your information on those networks down low so that it's not detectable, and just have the backdoor capability to get in, and then do something when the need arises.

And so far, the apparent need has not yet arisen.

A key step in the second stage was the compromise of Microsoft's Active Directory. Gaining administrative control enables bad actors to pose as legitimate IT users, enabling the authentication using valid credentials, and to create new, though bogus accounts, undetected. Threat actors are then free to move throughout an organization's IT systems posing as a legitimate user, alert-free. This, of course, presented a huge roadblock to detecting the bad actor once s/he was inside.

While the Active Directory hacks complicated detection, it's not an uncommon part of an advanced persistent threat. There is, however, one truly remarkable element within this attack, which is the modification of the software build process.

Most APTs go after source code. These guys got right into the compile stage, which is the last place anyone would look, in part because no one would suspect that an attacker would embrace the "20 on a scale of 10" level of difficulty and in part, because very few folks these days can read actual programming languages versus scripts. Again, as Mandia has now warned, the implications of such a portable vector suggest many more breaches of this nature in the near term.

Theresa Payton, the former White House Chief Information Officer, opines, "This vulnerability allowed the nefarious cyber operatives to create what we refer to in the industry as 'God access or a God door,' basically giving them rights to do anything they want in stealth mode."

Richard Clarke, the first U.S. "cyber czar" and current Chairman of Good Harbor cybersecurity notes: "This is not just about an espionage attack. This is about something called preparation of the battlefield, where they are now able, in the time of crisis, to eat the software in thousands of U.S. companies."

This brings me to Journalist David E. Sanger's observation that: "If a hacker went into your computer system just to read your email, that's pure espionage. But what people discovered over time, was that the same computer code that enabled them to break into somebody's system would also enable them to manipulate that system. If the network was connected to an electric power grid, to a gas pipeline, to a water distribution system, to a nuclear centrifuge plant, you might be able to manipulate the data and cause havoc in those systems. And that's much more than mere espionage."

IIOT/IOT AND CYBER-PHYSICAL THREATS

Is the nefarious activity at Oldsmar, Florida – where in early February, an (unknown) threat actor remotely accessed a computer for the water treatment system (using TeamViewer, a very commonly used program by hundreds of thousands of organizations world-wide, facilitating remote trouble-shooting by tech support folks) and increased the amount of sodium hydroxide (a.k.a. lye) used to control acidity in the water, to 100 times the normal level – connected with the cyberattacks on SolarWinds, Microsoft, and Accellion?

ICS/SCADA vulnerabilities climb into the billions as our connected IIoT empire expands beyond simple math, and likely presents the greatest threat to the United States since, well, ever.

In fact, Accenture Security reports that "Indirect attacks against weak links in the supply chain now account for 40% of security breaches." "Now," as in, today, and not as in, tomorrow.

Drilling a bit deeper into the threat to IIoT devices controlling water systems, we find that of the approximately 54,000 drinking water systems in the United States, almost all rely on some type of remote access to monitor and/or administer, most are unattended, underfunded, and don't have 24/7 IT oversight.

A majority of these facilities, mirroring the majority of electric grid systems, have not separated operational technology (pumps, controls, switches, and levers) from IT systems – inviting island hopping through an endpoint monitoring and control workaround. And, water systems present an attractive target because while the country can live without electricity for a while, the same thesis does not apply to drinking water.

We witnessed a water system attack back in 2013, when we saw bad actors breaking into systems that controlled the Bowman Dam in Rye, New York, and could have gotten access to its controls if it hadn't been offline at that moment for maintenance. Three years later, our DOJ charged an Iranian national with the attack, rationalizing that he worked for a company tied to the Iranian Revolutionary Guard Corps.

And, in 2020, the Treasury Department sanctioned a Russian government institution accused of having created a destructive campaign called Triton, which targets public and private IIoT.

So the threats are very real, the next set of attack vectors have been nested in over 250,000 networks, including countless industrial control systems, and no one in the business of cybersecurity seems to know what to do about them.

A few eye-opening IoT/IIoT stats:

> The 4th Industrial revolution (the IoT device market) is poised to reach $1.1 trillion by 2026 (Fortune Business Insights), a breathtaking 24.7% Compound Annual Growth Rate (CAGR). The significance of the CAGR is that it captures the attention of most VCs who stand in line for CAGR opportunities like that one, so even in these artifically constrained investment moments of pause and see, money will pour into this space, assuring a rapid and continuous growth rate and scale. It could well be described as the enemy of good security at the same time because growth in digitization drags hybrid and raw Cloud computing along with it. Cloud is one of our weakest links in cybersecurity already - imagine the impact of millions of new instantiations.

IDC data estimates that 152,200 IoT devices will be connected every minute by 2025. The math says that at this rate, that by 2025, nearly 80 billion (79,996,320,000) devices are forecast to be connected annually.

Ericsson forecasts 3.5 billion cellular IoT connections by 2023 due in part to 5G.

A Deloitte study reveals that digital transformation is a top strategic objective for 94% of executives; 85% have IoT project budgets.

Ponemon, Symantec, and Netscout report that fewer than 20% of risk professionals can identify a majority of their organization's IoT devices, 75% of infected devices in IoT attacks are routers, and IoT devices are typically attacked within five minutes.

And 55% of companies surveyed don't require third-party IoT supply-chain provider security and privacy compliance.

The amazing thing about the laws of large numbers can be most easily digested by examining the compounding effect of chess board moves. After the first move by both opponents, there are about 400 different board setups that may occur. Think about that - one move each - 400 new board setups. After the second move, that number escalates to 197,000. After each player's third move, 120 million game variations will have occurred. After four moves, you get 10 to the 120th.

That would be 10 plus 120 trailing zeros. That's just stupid crazy.

Almost twice the number of atoms in the observable universe.

IIoT/IoT may be an Industrial Revolution, but it will, without a doubt, bring a second Cybersecurity Revolution as well.

One for which we are uniquely unprepared to deal.

Cyber-physical systems (CPSs) are a new category of risk that include systems that orchestrate sensing, computation, control, networking, and analytics to interact with the physical world (including humans).

They are the heart-beat of all connected devices where security spans both the cyber and physical worlds.

The open source TCP/IP stacks, which are used to manage most of these devices, impacted more than 150 vendors and millions of their products in healthcare during the first quarter of 2021.

Internet of Medical Things (IoMT) brings this concept into hyper-focus where it is easy to imagine pacemakers and defibrillators being attacked and their users and/or providers held for hostage.

Gartner predicts that the financial impact of CPS attacks resulting in fatal casualties will reach over $50 billion by 2023.

With OT, smart buildings, smart cities, connected cars, and autonomous vehicles evolving, a focus on operational resilience needs an infusion of urgency.

CISA and the FBI have already increased the details provided around threats to critical infrastructure-related systems.

Now, CEOs will no longer be able to plead ignorance or hide behind insurance policies.

Gartner predicts that by 2024, liability for cyber-physical security incidents will begin to pierce the corporate veil for CEO protection.

Maybe after a few disasters and massive wrongful death lawsuits, the C-suite will finally come to realize that this "security business" is actually their first priority, and not just one of the top few threats.

In addition to all of that exposure, on March 20, 2021, the discovery of a new variant of Mirai was reported that leverages security flaws in D-Link, Netgear, and SonicWall devices, and since early February, this variant has targeted six known vulnerabilities, along with three previously unknown ones to infect systems and add them to a botnet network; a botnet is a collection of web connected devices including servers, PCs, mobile devices, and IoT devices, that are infected and controlled by shared malware. A system commonly becomes part of a botnet without the user even realizing it. These hijacked devices can be used to carry out distributed denial-of-service attacks, steal data, send spam – or even remotely access the local network of a device.

More than 60 variants of Mirai have been observed in the last 90 days and most of them take advantage of known or unknown vulnerabilities in IIoT devices. The latest attacks are based on a recent variant of Mirai's source code, targeting some additional, newly discovered vulnerabilities in IIoT devices.

Six high-alert CVE's had been issued months before the attack, yet no patches had been applied.

GEO-POLITICAL POWER SHIFTS

In Ukraine, in December 2015, the Russian Sandworm Team hacked into the Ukrainian power grid, and took it down. The Russians gained access to the connected IT network, from which they pivoted to the SCADA portion of the network, and manipulated the ICS controls to shut down power in Kiev.

This attribution is not speculation, Russia took credit publicly.

XENOTIME, and its association with the TRITON malware, is now the most dangerous IIoT threat actor, targeting a specific safety instrumented component within industrial control systems, designed to protect health and environmental safety in industrial settings.

Manipulated SIS leads to loss of life. The bar has now been raised.

Cybersecurity researchers are also convinced that Russian operators, like the Sandworm Team, have attacked and embedded malware in western ICS systems over the last few years, preparing for future attacks.

What are they waiting for? A really good reason.

Russian cyber operations represent a very real and current threat, and Russian intelligence services will continue to view corporations, governments, and civil society as viable targets for espionage and disinformation operations.

Because it is working.

Lat last year we saw a massive buildup of 90,000 plus troops at the Ukraine border as Russia signaled their distaste over U.S. foreign policy declarations that criticized and sanctioned Russia for using energy exports as a political weapon against eastern European counties while shipping natural gas and heating oil directly to Germany.

Piling on that display of territorial strength, Russia blamed the European Union for the migrant crisis on the border between Belarus and Poland that is pushing millions of refugees into Belarus.

These apparently small and remote, localized and physical conflicts are critical to our foreign policy thinking, in that every one of them is backed by an implied cyberattack.

Backed by considerable strength in cyber-operations, Russia is easily able to demonstrate its skill in the arena of hacked U.S. pipelines and distribution systems and is unmotivated to hold back. We have an opportunity to shift our foreign policy under these conditions, but because of the very conditions themselves, find ourselves cornered within our own strategic determinations and are unlikely to do so at this late hour.

Which will also mean for the Ukrainians, a cold winter and an escalation of repatriation, and a suddenly crowded country with millions competing for limited supplies of food and shelter. And the war we are all now in.

Our foreign policy decisions are having the same effect in China and India, Pakistan and Afghanistan. The near-term future may be murky, but the single and central unifier throughout all is the cyberattack.

All of the campaigns discussed here have been active through 2021 and the pace with which these have progressed is unprecedented. These threats are not hypothetical.

They are real, clear, and very present.

Without a major shift in our defense philosophy, we will remain as sitting ducks. We will need to work much more transparently with Federal agencies upon the tenet of collective defense, which will enable organizations to operate with visibility into threat intelligence, not only from their own networks but from the accumulated knowledge of multiple communities so as to discover active threats much more quickly.

And the question over what to do about them once discovered, will find answers in the tenets of active defense or, dare I say it, offensive security.

Bringing this all together will require bold courage on the part of politicians and the private community, many of which will be naturally reluctant to share proprietary information, or work together without regard for private gain.

But that is what happens in war-time, and the reluctance underscore's the reality that it has been over 75 years since we have collectively faced an existential threat on a global scale.

OUT OF CONTROL

In the coming months, you should assume a continuation of supply chain attacks, and an increase in both purse money and frequency of ransomware attacks leveraging the open doors left in the wake of the Exchange server attack flood.

We should also see a large-scale ICS attack, perhaps not on U.S. soil but designed similarly to that of Petya/NotPetya, and released in the wild to test another self-directed attack of massive proportion.

We will likely continue slow progress toward a public and private cybersecurity defense partnership, impacted by conflicting political agendas, internal squabbling, and hierarchical directives along with in-creased and emboldened rhetoric from both Russia and China as they flex their newly affirmed cyber-superiority with fresh global threats and expanded disruption.

THE FUTURE

Future growth will expose more point-solution competition from a collective of new players in the cybersecurity marketplace fueled by large injections of venture capital into startups and early stage companies.

These companies will bring AI and ML technologies to the automated detection and defense stage, and greater progress and competitive se-paration from Chinese dominance of the global Quantum market with the first public announcement of a quantum crypto break, as quantum computers will be able to demonstrate breaking the traditional public key crypto.

As more people have adopted the work-from-home protocols, employees will take cybersecurity shortcuts for convenience, and insufficiently secured personal devices and routers, along with the transfer of sensitive information over unsecured or unsanctioned channels, will continue to play an igniting role in data breaches and leaks.

We will need and might see, a stronger emphasis on detection of cybersecurity threats in the future, as we all now know that protection alone has not defeated the biggest and most damaging cybersecurity threats in history. Advanced, unified, and extended detection and response vendors should see a majority of the spotlight in the next few quarters. Detection and response, when it comes to threats characterized by unprecedented levels of sophistication, professionalism, and maliciousness, will dominate the market.

We may also see an acceleration in the adoption of AI-based and machine learning Cloud SIEM tools, and an increase in automated threat hunting and orchestration, enabling the collection of cybersecurity threats in real-time.

Progress toward the fourth Industrial Revolution driven by the rise of 5G technology, will provide more, not fewer, opportunities for cyber attackers to take over systems and networks. And popular mobile-only designs will intensify the threat and stimulate the further elimination of perimeters while pushing increased cloud adoption, creating an additional extension of the threat landscape.

One that will become even more difficult to defend.

Segregating un-secured IIoT and 5G-enabled devices from the rest of the network will be preached as a common best practice, but fewer hygiene organizations will be able to comply, as the gap between trained and untrained cybersecurity personnel will continue to widen.

Phishing will keep plaguing businesses and the pandemic will remain a popular theme for PsyOps-intensive phishing campaigns, designed to lure information-deprived users with the announcement of a new vaccine, a shift in lockdown protocols, or a surge in new infections. Embracing improved and innovative online education within a curated program for increased situational awareness may begin a trend toward a long overdue culture of cybersecurity readiness.

Fileless attacks and instances of business process compromises will also increase. These threats are able to fly beneath the radar of conventional SIEM solutions and usually succeed. They will continue to do so.

The next few years should begin an inflection point for edge computing. This, of course, will further expand the attack surface and extend the opportunity for attackers to gain entry through various entry points of the extended architecture. Businesses will generally not have insight into every device being connected to this extended network, and will thus create increased cybersecurity risks without understanding the threats imposed by the new topologies.

Containers, Kubernetes, and micro-segmentation will all be rushed to adoption, resulting in increased pressure on the human factor to optimize configuration performance, at which we will fail at a greater rate than in the past.

Why?

Because we have a prefrontal cortex.

HUMAN FACTORS

The pre-frontal cortex is the epicenter of our cognitive horsepower, and delivers our ability to focus on the task at hand. Under normalized conditions, it runs on autopilot and we power right through mundane tasks. But in times of abnormal conditions, and intense stress, our prefrontal cortex begins firing on cylinders it doesn't possess and causes us to focus on the step-by-step details of our performance, seeking an optimal outcome and, as a result, disrupting what would have otherwise been fluid and natural.

It translates to an increase in insider threat for which we are not prepared.

Unintentional insider threat will increase owing largely to the gap in properly trained resources and the very pressing need for every business to train and educate all employees in the fundamentals of cybersecurity risk associated with each emerging market trend.

Predicting that humans will continue to represent a larger threat in the future is easy.

Not only do we not know enough about risk-management and cybersecurity basics, we are more highly pressured than in the past and as a result will begin making more stress-driven mistakes in critical areas like configuration management, policy distribution, and even in forensics and discovery.

Complicating the landscape are factors like increased complexity in networks, compliance mandates and regulations, an increase in M&A

activity resulting in the combination of cybersecurity threat defense capabilities without actual integration, and an increase in the general malaise and uncertainty about our abilities to compete on the battlefield.

So, the resulting market messaging will confuse and deflect while our adversaries continue to improve, educate, and tool up, and we will continue to fall further back on progress in education and workforce development, on the discipline required of hygienic correctness, and on the recognition of the human factor's role in cybersecurity efficacy.

There is hope, but it's harder to find than in the past.

RANSOMWARE

Following on the heels of a harrowing 2020 and 2021, the landscape became littered with even more detritus, left behind by a furious onslaught of ransomware hits, raising the stakes, and targeting critical infrastructure as the Kremlin and Beijing continue to test both the strength and cunning of his attack teams and the preparedness and resilience of our cybersecurity defense teams.

Though it may seem like a while ago now, with all of the mainstream media coverage it received, the Colonial Pipeline attack was announced on May 7, 2021, and the follow-on news focused on whether Colonial would pay the ransom or refuse to cooperate with the thieves. As gasoline lines began to form all along the eastern seaboard, it became clear to the cybersecurity community that Colonial's OT was infected as well as their IT networks.

Though they never admitted it.

It also became clear to those panicked and stranded in long gasoline lines filling plastic garbage bags with gas, that cyberattacks had suddenly become visceral and very kinetic.

Average walk-around citizens now knew what a cyber-attack felt like and most who shared their views on social media were not anxious for more.

Refusing to describe either the origins or extent of the attack, Colonial knuckled under, and after only one day, ponied up $5 million.

Whether one day of deliberation is enough to convince analysts that the pipeline side of the business had been compromised is speculative, but it is pretty compelling evidence to most. If the OT side had been left operational, the inability to bill for product delivery via their ERP integration would have not been near enough to warrant such a payout or any at all.

Subsequently, the FBI managed to showcase their skills at crypto-currency tracing and hacking crypto-wallets and clawed back $2.3 million that had not yet been distributed out through the myriad of blockchain connections that the dark Websters use to camouflage their laundering.

In this case, DarkSide.

Nonetheless, as we have repeatedly pointed out through our outreach, this attack was not about money, but rather about a demonstration of vulnerability and the ease with which a foreign national could bring down a key distribution system upon which we depend for every day convenience and facility.

Not to say, the money wasn't part of the deal. It just wasn't part of Vladimir's deal.

The ransom is the payout to the teams within DarkSide that the Kremlin directs to conduct these clandestine cyber-attacks, and Putin is happy that they get paid from outside his own circle.

Many people are unaware that Putin owns 4.5% of the natural gas producer Gazprom, has a 37% stake in the Russian oil company Surgutneftegas, and owns 50% of the Swiss oil-trader Gunvor. Using their most recent market capitalizations, Putin's combined ownership stakes would give him a personal net worth of $70 billion, and likely closer to $200 billion, as Hermitage Capital Management's CEO Bill Browder told the Senate Judiciary Committee in 2020.

That either puts him at 14th on the global rich list, just ahead of Steve Ballmer and Carlos Slim, and only $27 billion behind Zuckerberg, or second, only behind Jeff Bezos. As the price of gas and oil have sky-rocketed in the past five months, it will not take him long to close that gap, or ascend above the Amazon mogul.

LESSONS LEARNED

What did we learn from Colonial?

- Don't connect your IT networks with your IIoT networks.

- Stop using legacy VPNs, and particularly those with a single password, absent multifactor authentication.

- Put someone in charge of information security and call her a CISO.

- Have a rehearsed and tested incident response and recovery plan in place.

- Call the FBI right away.

Less than 30 days later, we saw JBS Foods get hit with a similar ransomware attack shutting down operations in Australia, Canada, and the United States, affecting thousands of workers.

How big a deal was that?

JBS is the world's largest meat supplier with more than 150 plants in 15 countries, employs more than 150,000 employees, and in the United States, it processes nearly one-quarter of our beef and one-fifth of our pork. Vegetarians didn't care all that much, but meat eaters got hit with immediate scarcity and increased prices, and many people who subsist on a McDonald's diet were severely impacted.

Again, this attack was social experimentation, and had little to do with the $11 million paid to the Russian crime-family. And, if anyone feels pretty good about their cybersecurity defenses and the degree to which their IT has been hardened against Ransomware attacks, please note that JBS spends more than $200 million annually on IT and cybersecurity while it employs more than 850 IT and cybersecurity professionals globally.

Though you may spend, spending alone won't get you to the Promised Land.

Quietly reported in the second week of June was another CI ransomware attack, this time on Sol Oriens, a subcontractor for the U.S. Department of Energy (DOE) that works on nuclear weapons with the National Nuclear Security Administration (NNSA).

REvil unabashedly takes credit for the attack with a message that claims, "The subcontractor did not take all necessary action to protect personal data of their employees and software development for partner companies. We hereby keep a right to forward all of the relevant documentation and data to military agencies of our choice, including all personal data of employees."

David Bishop, CISO of Trustwave, offered that we need "more serious repercussions" for this type of attack. "We're seeing advanced adversaries getting much bolder with who they are attacking, how they are blackmailing the targeted organization, and how they are monetizing their stolen goods."

Most of these organized groups are financially motivated, but if these types of attackers shift their motivation from monetary to malicious, we should expect severe real-world outcomes." Bishop continued. "We've only seen the tip of the iceberg in terms of the real-world effects with the cyber-attacks on JBS and Colonial Pipeline. The public and private sectors need to closely co-ordinate on what we can accomplish in terms of hard legal or offensive action to combat these threats – otherwise, these adversaries will continue to attack at will.

Then, in late September, New Cooperative, an Iowa-based agriculture supply chain was hit by a ransomware attack, and has refused to pay the $5.9 million ransom demand from BlackMatter, the heir to the DarkSide crew that carried out the Colonial Pipeline operation earlier this year.

How did they get in?

BlackMatter brute-forced hundreds of employee credentials left exposed by poor password management, and researchers discovered that password "chicken1" was used more than 10 times among the company's 120 employees. Passwords used by some of the co-op's top executives were also compromised, and, in total, researchers found more than 650 instances of breached credentials.

Stop using passwords and start using MFA is starting to sound as basic as don't run with scissors.

GAMING

Adding additional fuel, the massive ($5 billion) gaming company Electronic Arts (EA) has also been hacked, during which game source code and related internal tools were stolen. The hackers, of course, made the announcement first, explaining that they managed to get away with the source code for FIFA 21, as well as code for its matchmaking server. The hackers also said they have obtained source code and tools for the Frostbite engine, which powers a number of EA games including Battlefield, Madden, Need for Speed, and others.

Getting in by first infiltrating one of the company's communication channels, and for just $10, the hackers purchased a cookie that allowed them to join the company's Slack channel. They then posed as an employee to convince at IT administrator to grant them authentication to get into the company's corporate network.

With the skyrocketed technology complexity that is now so prevalent across all market segments, we now have so many ways to get into a target's network, it appears impossible to keep adversaries out.

If this were golf match, I would have picked up after 7.

This attack highlights the vulnerabilities created by workplace communication technologies, which have exploded in popularity during the pandemic. We continue to rapidly adopt new technologies without any vetting or planning. Combine that with the switch to remote workspaces, and we have created brand new ways for cybercriminals to target organizations, yet very few companies have been able to adjust to the new reality.

The theft of source code will create a host of problems for the company, primarily because FIFA 21 has its own virtual currency, which itself is in high demand.

Game source code is highly proprietary and sensitive intellectual property that is the heartbeat of a company's service or offering. Exposing this data is life-threatening and we have no idea at this point how this attack will ultimately impact the sustainability of the company's gaming services down the line.

While the motivations of the hackers appear to be strictly financial, the impact on EA's reputation could be serious. If, as many players suspect, the company has intentionally designed FIFA, one of its most popular titles, so that players who purchase coins have a better chance of winning matches and advancing their teams than players who do not, it could prove disastrous to the game's reputation and popularity.

About $1.5B worth of FIFA coins were purchased by players in 2020.

Because EA game coins are bought and sold by players using real-world currency on unregulated market places like buyfifacoins.com, the hackers could be trying to attract the attention of organized hacker groups like China's Apt 41. With the source code, certificates, and API keys in hand, Apt 41 could use them to mine coins and sell them in a process known as Gold Farming.

In 2015, the FBI arrested a group that had allegedly mined and sold $15 to $18M worth of this virtual currency by using vulnerabilities found in the game. Making profit off the in-game currency would be one of the most likely interests for the cybercriminals interested in purchasing the source code.

Access to the source would also allow someone to understand the game's functionality, its servers, and logic, as well as undercover any secret algorithms and bypass anticheat technologies. With this knowledge, hackers could easily mine and sell the in-game currency.

The bad guys lifted 780 Gigs in total, which also includes all of the proprietary EA frameworks and software development kits (SDKs). As is often the case, these attacks are after one of the big four "P's." PII, PCI. PHI or IP.

And in this case, the EA Intellectual Property (IP) is immediately fungible.

AIR TRANSPORTATION

Air India's tag line, "Truly Indian," suddenly popped into the news in June when they announced a massive cyber-attack by the Chinese nation-state threat actor, APT41.

Group-IB, with their Threat Intelligence & Attribution system being named one of the best in class by Gartner, Forrester, and IDC, are leading the investigation and have said that the current attack may have been a supply chain attack targeting SITA, but it is not the same attack the airline announced in May.

SITA is a multinational information technology company providing IT and telecommunication services to the air transportation industry.

The potential ramifications of this incident for the entire airline industry and carriers that might yet discover traces of the malware known as ColunmTK, based on the names of command-and-control (C2) server domains in their networks, are significant.

Group-IB's analysis has now revealed that at least since February 23, an infected device inside Air India's network (named "SITASERVER4") communicated with a server hosting Cobalt Strike payloads dating all the way back to December 11, 2020.

Following this initial compromise, the attackers are said to have established persistence and obtained passwords in order to pivot laterally to the broader network with the goal of gathering information inside the local network.

These back doors enable long-term, transparent data flows that appear to be legitimate under today's available technical scrutiny.

This is what is likely going on right now in Federal networks and hundreds of other commercial networks following the Microsoft and SolarWinds attacks.

That earlier breach involved personally identifiable and PCI data reaching back to August 26, 2011, and continuing on through February

3, 2021. Those stolen records contained names, dates of birth, contact information, passport information, ticket information, Star Alliance, and Air India frequent flyer data, as well as credit card data.

FireEye's Mandiant, which is assisting SITA with the incident response efforts, has since determined that the attack was highly sophisticated and that the tactics, techniques, and procedures (TTPs) and compromise indicators point to a single well-known entity.

Group-IB claims proof that a server in Air India's network was hacked first, after it had established a connection to SITA's network.

We will watch how this expands within the airline industry and the interconnections with SITA. Once again, our network complexity creates substantial opportunities for digital explorers with bad intent.

TRUE 20 YEARS AGO; TRUE TODAY

All of these supply-chain, CI, and ransomware cyberattacks are reminiscent of the findings in a 20–year-old report entitled, "Protecting America's Critical Infrastructures: How Secure Are Government Computer Systems?" presented to the Congressional Subcommittee on Oversight and Investigations back in April of 2001, that offered in part, "America has long depended on a complex of systems – or critical infrastructures – to assure the delivery of services vital to its national defense, economic prosperity, and social well-being.

These infrastructures include telecommunications, water supplies, electric power, oil and gas delivery and storage, banking and finance, transportation, and vital human and government services."

Aka, a target-rich environment.

And the report made the following recommendations: "Identify the nodes and networks that should receive robust cyber and physical vulnerability assessments; conduct near-term risk management assessments; justify funding requests for high-priority security enhancement measures in the areas of physical security, information system security, industrial security, emergency preparedness, counter-intelligence, counter-terrorism; and review actual business processes to better understand and improve the efficiencies of its organization's functions and information technology architectures."

20 years ago.

Too little, too late, and maybe not at all.

CHAPTER 4

The Connected World

As the wave of cyber-crime and cyber-espionage rages on across all industries globally, on a more personal level, vulnerabilities in our connected world are expanding as well. CVE-2021-33887 is a published vulnerability in the Android Verified Boot (AVB) process for all devices relying upon Android operating systems.

Like, for example, the Peloton, which has not been a stranger to front-page news stories ever since reports of children and a pet being pulled, pinned, and entrapped under the rear roller of the Tread+ treadmill, leading to the death of one child.

McAfee researchers described a worst-case scenario where an attacker could boot the Peloton with a modified image to gain elevated privileges and then leverage those privileges to establish a reverse shell, granting the attacker unfettered root access on the bike remotely. The hacker could then tamper with the product at any point from construction to warehouse to delivery, installing a backdoor into the Android tablet that comes with the bike without the end user knowing.

An attacker could also walk up to a Peloton bike installed in a gym and perform an attack, gaining root access to these devices for later use.

While topical, because of all the high-profile people who use Pelotons, including the POTUS and first lady, the AVB vulnerability isn't unique to Peloton. Any and all Android bootloader security settings need to be configured properly by the manufacturer, or a bad actor can gain complete control of the bootloader and the device, whatever it may be.

DOI: 10.1201/9781003331773-5

In the case of Peloton, however, their camera, microphone, and local network access make it a particularly attractive target.

In our new WFH world, those elements easily serve as a pivot point to access other devices connected to the home network and tangentially, the enterprise network connected through the same router. The threat landscape then expands to include covertly listening in on virtual meetings and other sensitive business conversations that now take place away from a centralized physical office location.

And further expansion can easily occur within any OT or IoT setting when the OS for a connected device is Android-based and connected to, for instance, an IoMT device in a hospital where many medical devices run on Android operating systems.

HEALTHCARE SCARES

It's only a matter of time before we start seeing increasing deadly attacks within our highly vulnerable healthcare providers.

To this exact point, Stillwater Medical Center was hit with a ransomware attack on June 13, 2021, and four months later, was still operating under electronic health record downtime as it attempted to bring its systems back online. The health system operates a number of care sites, specialist offices, hospitals, and clinics in Oklahoma.

In the immediate wake of the attack, Stillwater experienced major disruptions to its phone systems, and patients were urged to call 911 instead of the hospital line. There were also reports of a broken online patient portal and associated email system.

A late update on June 15, 2021, two days following the attack, indicated that the phone service was working only intermittently throughout the entire health system.

The Stillwater attack occured directly after another cyberattack on two University of Florida Health hospitals, whose systems remained offline and inaccessible forweeks after the attack. The Villages Regional Hospital with over 130,000 residents in their retirement community was attacked alongside Leesburg Hospital, on May 31, 2021, and both were forced to operate under under downtime procedures following the incident.

After all of these attacks, hospital clinicians temporarily began documenting patient care with pen and paper to keep up with patient needs in a downtime environment.

The increased physical danger arises out of the absence of reliable and immediate electronic healthcare record (EHR) access, which puts patients at risk for unverifiable allergies or potential drugs to avoid. Clinicians reported that the system outages caused some patients to either miss medications or receive the wrong prescription.

The hospital staff had to call pharmacies directly to verify patient prescription histories. There werealso reports of staff inadvertently matching patients with the wrong lab chart. The outages also caused long delays in the receipt of lab reports.

Further from home, the Ireland Health Service Executive (HSE), Ireland's largest public health system, suffered a significant ransomware attack that took down all of their networks nationwide down on May 14, 2021. It took nearly four months for servers and devices to be fully restored.

One month after the attack, HSE continued to require patients to bring their PHI with them to the emergency department, including medical records and patient chart numbers, medications, and any previous discharge summaries. The impact on efficient patient care was immeasurable, as only urgent care for life-threatening conditions was provided through the emergency center, and all out-patient care wascanceled until systems could be recovered.

The radiology and medical imaging departments across all sites appear to have been the hardest hit by the attack. Immediately following the attack, appointments for those departments were canceled.

> "Notwithstanding the substantial technical recovery and improved operational capacity, it's evident that information and communications technology (ICT) and clinical communication systems fall short of what is required to work safely and deliver care at an acceptable level of risk," HSE Chief Clinical Officer Colm Henry, MD, explained to staff.

> "In most instances workarounds remain in place," he added. "Major ICT systems such as NIMIS, Apex and ICM have been restored, but not to the level required to provide system integration and seamless clinical communication. It remains the case that recovery of ICT systems is not synonymous with service recovery."

As the HSE recovery team worked around the clock, uploading backlogs and reconciling patient records, and cleansing and rebuilding systems, they discovered an alarming number of systems and devices that were destroyed beyond repair.

In other global news, it took nearly one month, following a ransomware attack that struck multiple hospitals of the Waikato District Health Board (DHB) in New Zealand, for IT team to bring IT services fully back online.

Clinicians operating using EHR downtime procedures used pen and paper to record patient interactions and had to hire hundreds of additional IT workers to assist with recovery efforts while refusing to pay the attackers' demands.

Months later, they were been able to restore only about 20% of its workstation network and just a little more than half of its servers.

Reports from on-site clinicians and staff members showed the cyberattack caused chaos at the impacted hospitals. Providers were unable to send x-ray images between departments, access patient notes, or access patient records.

In the first half of 2021 alone, ransomware attacks have brought down the network of multiple other providers, including Scripps Health; Rehoboth McKinley Christian Hospital in Gallup, New Mexico; Arizona-based Cochise Eye and Laser; St. Margaret's Health - Spring Valley; and Allergy Partners in North Carolina, among others.

About 1,000 healthcare providers have been affected by ransomware attacks every week, reflecting a 7% cumulative increase on a month-over-month basis.

In other words, not only is it not slowing down, it is increasing dramatically.

While the Department of Homeland Security's CISA and NIST continue to publish and stress the adoption of best practice defense and mitigation measures, much more can and has to be done by our federal agencies to step onto this battlefield.

Because the threats to human life elevate the conversation to a national security level issue, and healthcare providers cannot alone defend themselves from this storm of incoming attacks.

Perhaps members of the federal cybersecurity team, John C. Inglis and Jen Easterly, will have an immediate impact on this sector with new support and a takeover of the cybersecurity infrastructure for healthcare providers.

Radical?

Indeed.

COFFEE MONEY

In May, 2021 the mortgage settlement giant First American Financial Corp. was discovered to be leaking more than 800 million documents, many containing sensitive PII/financial data, related to real estate transactions dating back 16 years.

In the second week of June, the SEC settled its investigation after First American agreed to pay a penalty of less than $500,000. Since they generate $6.2 billion in revenue, the penalty was as insignificant to First American as coffee money. Without fiscal consequences or ramifications, why should anyone spend millions on cybersecurity technologies?

A $500K fine is simply a no-brainer, a minor risk transfer.

This is the equivalent of the fox in charge of the hen house. If the SEC can't insist on penalties that are commensurate to the crime, it will be hard to escape the rinse and repeat cycle for cyber-crime in the financial sectors.

Not because the Wall Street leaders are bad actors, but rather because the same folks are great business-people.

UNINTENDED TRAPS

The Open Design Alliance (ODA) is a nonprofit organization that creates open-source SDKs for engineering applications, including CAD, GIS, building and construction, product lifecycle management (PLM), and IoT. Itswebsite claims 1,200 member companies worldwide, and its products are used by folks like Siemens, Microsoft, Bentley, and Epic Games.

It turns out that ODA's Drawings SDK, which is designed to provide access to all data design files, is affected by several vulnerabilities that can be exploited by convincing the targeted user to open a specially crafted file.

The vulnerabilities, rated high and medium severity, can be exploited to cause a denial of service (DoS) condition, execute arbitrary code, or obtain potentially sensitive information by getting the targeted user to open specially crafted DWG or DGN files with an application that uses the SDK.

ODA, in defense, noted that in order to be able to take complete control of a system, an attacker would need to chain one of the code execution vulnerabilities with a privilege escalation flaw.

So, it's not a real big cybersecurity threat.

Except it is.

That the same technique was leveraged through SolarWinds' vulnerabilities, and that cyberattack didn't turn out so well for the good guys.

The South Korean Atomic Energy Research Institute (KAERI) was hacked on May 14, 2021 by the NoKo bad guys, aka the Kimsuky group. CISA has recognized the group as a global intelligence gathering team that has targeted South Korean COVID-19 vaccine researchers and nuclear reactors.

The group often uses phishing to mimic websites like Gmail and Outlook. Then they install an Android and Windows backdoor called AppleSeed to collect information.

A vulnerability in a VPN used by KAERI allowed access to one of the agency's servers before they could detect, block the IP addresses, and install security patches. The KAERI network was breached using an email address from President Moon Jae-in's former advisor, Moon Chung-in, that was acquired during a 2018 Kimsuky-attributed cyberattack, almost three years earlier.

Proving once again that just because nothing apparently happens following a cyberattack, doesn't mean there won't be downstream damage. Imagine bringing your cyber-insurer a claim for a hack that occurred three years ago when your computing environment was completely different and multiple risk assessments had been conducted since.

Officials fear that the leaking of information pertaining to nuclear technology, like reactors and fuel rods, could pose security risks, and this attack may be part of a larger ongoing campaign. Malwarebytes, in early June, reported several attacks on South Korean universities, government officials, and companies in South Korea, and attributed them to Kimsuky.

When we don't hear about these attacks in our news feeds, we often feel like the world is not as scary as we thought, but we'd be wrong. There is more cybersecurity action occurring in the South China Sea than in all of Western Europe as four countries jockey for position on the global stage. The end may well usher in the next stage of our global relationships with a bang, over a whisper, and whichever way it goes, U.S. interests are closely tied to all four countries.

WATER EVERYWHERE

A June 2021 survey conducted by the Water Information Sharing and Analysis Center (Water-ISAC) and the Water Sector Coordinating

Council tried to assess the state of cyber-preparedness among 606 water and wastewater utilities.

These represented approximately 52,000 community water systems and 16,000 wastewater systems in the United States, and the general findings were that the water industry demonstrated a range of cybersecurity preparedness, ranging from a little to none.

Little to none.

Many of the utilities were self-assessed as "subject to economic disadvantages typical of rural and urban communities," while others didn't have access to a cybersecurity workforce at all.

Regardless of the excuse, almost all of these utilities are struggling to maintain and replace infrastructure and comply with safe and clean water regulations, while still being able to maintain their necessary levels of profitability.

More than 60% of water utilities say they have not fully identified IT assets in their networks, and only a little more than 21% of those utilities said they are working to do so. Roughly 70% said they have not fully identified all OT assets and fewer than a quarter are working to do so.

Why did it take a near-miss in Oldsmar, Florida, following an earlier discovered attempt at poisoning a water treatment plant in Oakland using the same TeamViewer vulnerability, before this essential lifeline came into focus as a critical infrastructure threat with national security implications?

About 64% of respondents said their utility does not employ a chief information security officer.

The aforementioned Oakland incident, which was previously unreported, is one of many of the hundreds of treatment plants that responded they were "not sure" if they had experienced an incident.

The Water-ISAC published a list of six older CVEs for its members on June 17, 2021, saying it was "aware of several reports of threat actors leveraging multiple vulnerabilities to exploit unpatched systems in the water and wastewater sector."

The continuing risk assessment and evaluation of our water and pipeline systems falls remarkably under the EPA and the TSA, neither of whom have experience dealing with cybersecurity issues nor enforcement authority over cybersecurity lapses.

Their purview is limited to best practice recommendations which are not followed by many. And in the case of energy, as a senior TSA official in 2019 testified to lawmakers, the office responsible for securing the nation's pipelines – the Surface Division in the Office of Security Policy and Industry Engagement – has only five full-time employees, none of whom are cybersecurity experts, to watch over 2 million miles of energy pipeline.

And just as we tried to turn the page on June, 2021, we learned that on the 21, another attack on a water district player was discovered. The Metropolitan Water District of Southern California (MWDSC) was hacked by Chinese-backed hackers leveraging security vulnerabilities in the Pulse Connect Secure appliances, namely their VPN, which is notoriously porous.

MWDSC provides water to 19 million people living in Los Angeles, Orange, Riverside, San Bernardino, San Diego, and Ventura counties.

GOODBYE VPN

Security analysts say dozens of other high-value entities that have not yet been named, were also targeted as part of the breach of Pulse Secure, which is used by many companies and governments for secure remote access to their networks.

Unnamed victims could number in the thousands.

Mandiant Threat Intelligence assesses that Chinese cyber espionage activity has demonstrated a higher tolerance for risk and is less constrained by diplomatic pressures than previously characterized by senior members of the White Housestaff.

CISA has repeatedly warned of the potential threats faced by U.S. government agencies, critical infrastructure entities, and other private sector organizations, related to vulnerabilities in certain Ivanti Pulse Connect Secure appliances, a widely used SSL remote access solution. The exploitation of these vulnerabilities could allow an attacker to place web shells on the appliance to gain persistent system access to the appliance operating the vulnerable software.

CISA and the folks at MITRE ATT&CK can warn until the cows come home, but if no one is listening, we will continue to watch takedowns by these attackers, now emboldened as they discover a target-rich environment of unpatched opportunities and unmanaged and unprotected IIoT network infrastructures.

AN ABSENCE OF ACCOUNTABILITY

There is no better example of multiple agency cluster dances than those we have seen in the aftermath of the Colonial breach. Here we had the Department of Energy with the sector-specific agency for cybersecurity incidents, and its Cybersecurity, Energy Security and Emergency Response (CESER) office, which managed response. CISA was tracking the attack and publishing regular bulletins to industry about guarding against ransomware. The FBI was investigating as well.

There have been several pushes in Congress over the years to clarify or shift responsibilities, but those bills ultimately failed.

We needn't care whether congressmen can't figure out how Facebook makes money, but we DO care that these same lawmakers continually insist upon looking the other way, rather than confess their ignorance and seek an understanding of the growing threats to our National Critical Infrastructure, and then pass some legislation that will anger people and rustle feathers, but will also impose rules and consequences for the continual brushing off of fiduciary responsibilities by our system operators.

Both public and private.

The heightened pace and frequency of supply chain and infrastructure attacks have pushed the topic out of the private professional domain and over into society as a whole. There is nothing like Eastern seaboard gas lines following aggressive moves by a new administration to redact the prior administration's rules on energy independence to incite the imagination of everyday citizens.

Whether that move is good or bad energy policy is up for debate, but what isn't debatable is the response from ordinary folks trying to go about their daily lives.

A REAL BUSINESS PROBLEM

Yes, this cybersecurity business is a real problem and not just some ethereal threat casting about in space, the existence of which rivals UFOs in terms of national interest or concern.

Colonial changed all of that, and a second act on JBS Foods brought the message home, not just to the constituency but to the White House and Congress as well.

The societal perception of cybersecurity before those two attacks was essentially fear, uncertainty, and doubt, and it was completely disconnected from the realities of addressing it. Society has treated cybersecurity like a strange black box, with maybe a pulsing blue light on top.

Security experts are treated as mythical knowledge priests, but held far more weirdly than doctors or chemists, as regular folks just don't comprehend what these people actually do. Corporations give their CISOs lots of serious money, they weave some incomprehensible computer science together, the board reads reports that no one understands and everyone prays that nothing bad happens on their watch.

Over the first half of 2021, we have so much breach data that says business decision-making related to cyber-risk is still seriously flawed and when disconnected from the realities of business impact, leads to serious business harm. Our executives are distracted by compliance, the latest hackers and their techniques, and how much they are spending on cybersecurity defense.

In addition, we have seen an increase in aggression and confidence on behalf of our adversaries. All of the serious strikes we have discussed in reviewing this past year have taken the zero-day concept to new heights and spawned a new level of maturity among threat actors.

Now that we are paying attention, we notice many more attacks on infrastructure, especially water supplies and the systems that manage them. Ransomware attacks have come into focus now that the voting public is witnessing firsthand the enormous pay-outs that were rarely seen even two years ago.

This now-thriving business model, as attested to by bad folks like DarkSide, reveal their dark web presence resembling a consumer products campaign with press releases, YouTube "how-to" videos, a full-on tech support desk, financial planning, payment processing, negotiation proxies, and user guides as bonuses.

DarkSide alone earned just under $100 million in 2021.

Their business model is now what is known as "ransomware as a service," in which the malware developer charges a user fee based on a sliding scale that runs 25% for any ransoms less than $500,000, and escalating down to 10% for ransoms over $5 million.

With that level of support, even small-time criminal franchisee syndicates and hackers with only mediocre computer capabilities can pose a national security threat.

WE NEED HELP

American journalist Megyn Kelly interviewed Putin in 2018 and pressed him on why Russia was looking the other way, while hackers actively interfered in the American election, so he tried to remind her that there was nothing to arrest them for.

"If they did not break Russian law, there is nothing to prosecute them for in Russia," Putin said. "You must finally realize that people in Russia live by Russian laws, not by American ones."

The federal government has awakened to cybersecurity threats, and the need for the Fed to step in and provide some centralized control over the theater. How and when they are able to organize to do this is anyone's guess, and while it is way too late for us to start catching up to our adversaries, we will always take late over never.

Setting aside the inadequate funding for cybersecurity R&D, we now have a few 90-day plans, an executive order that is stressing Zero Trust and compliance mandates, new blood in senior positions within the security hierarchy, and some very talented folks in positions of authority.

Some wise man once said that our single greatest talent in America is creating bureaucracy, but we actually did some other things too.

Among them, we managed to create a weapon of mass destruction from some loose atomic science in only 27 months, and in eight short years we went from walking around on earth to walking around on the moon – and returning back.

We created tons of electronic, computer, medical, space, automotive, sustainable agricultural, and transportation breakthroughs, and we even created Google.

We have some of the brightest and best cybersecurity practitioners working hard to create innovative software, network, and hardware solutions to very specific and difficult security challenges. We are rushing to apply AI and machine learning to these products and creating breakthroughs in hard problems on a daily basis.

We have created a technologically dependent digital world where the United States is the most advanced in terms of adoption of the technology for advances in science and medicine, construction and telecommunications, biology and chemistry, mathematics, and engineering and as a result, we have wrapped ourselves in the glassiest of glass houses (to quote (ret.) General Keith Alexander).

We operate the controls at great risk.

CHAPTER 5

Cybersecurity Problems Are Hard Problems

L ooking back to the spring of 2019, a multinational manufacturing company named Norsk Hydro, a big international player in the global aluminum manufacturing supply chain got seriously hacked.

Lacking a corporate website, they had to use their Facebook account to notify folks, and of their 160 offices globally, most had to conduct everyday business without any digital infrastructure – they communicated via fax, pen, and paper.

The culprit?

LockerGoga, a ransomware strain that exhibits some interesting behaviors, including the ability to spawn different processes in order to accelerate the file encryption in the system, its execution depends upon launching from a privileged account, it creates multiple slave processes on the endpoints to encrypt its target files, and then it locks all users out by changing all credentials to dead destinations.

A month prior, a huge French IT services company called Altran was hit and completely crippled by the same ransomware.

Altran never said a word. To anyone.

As a result, not a word emerged in the media about LockerGoga. And consequently, not one cybersecurity product vendor flagged the file as malicious. Immediately following the Norsk attack, two U.S. chemical manufacturing companies were attacked using the same malware, without subsequent disclosure.

DOI: 10.1201/9781003331773-6

There are so many gaps and holes in our cybersecurity eco-system, it is often hard to decide where to start. Non-disclosure however is a great candidate.

Contrary to some popular sentiment, our cybersecurity vendor community does an admirable job of issuing patches for vulnerabilities rapidly after they are discovered and generally offer full disclosure around exploits.

But if attack victims keep this stuff secret, we are allowing the threats to continue without the ability to warn downstream victims against similar attacks. We need to stop worrying selfishly about reputational impact and start publishing these things as soon as possible following an event, along with technical details around the attack vector. It is no longer unusual for an organization to be breached and in fact, those who haven't yet been breached are beginning to appear conspicuous by their absence.

The United Kingdom has a National Cyber Security Centre's Information Sharing Partnership and it is working well, generating the expected dividends, fostering active cooperation and effectively building out a practical and useful threat library.

We need to follow its act.

It is long past the time to continue allowing individual organizations to make their own decisions about what is to be reported and when. We need global requirements and standards for private disclosure along with the free flow of technical information to trusted examiners.

But we also need to assure a quid-pro-quo for businesses who conform.

This must take the form of a government shield, protecting the reporting company from blow-back in the form of class-action lawsuits and claims of contributory negligence, along with a return of capital in the event a ransomware payment must be made (ala, Colonial Pipeline, who will soon be facing both legal issues amid scores of class action suits).

Had not Colonial paid that ransom demand, their OT systems were surely compromised and no transportation fuel would have flowed to all of those destinations up and down the eastern seaboard. It begs the question of where the line should be drawn. Is the Colonial attack, an attack on a private company, or an attack on our national security?

If the latter, immediate Government intervention is not just appropriate, it is required. It is after all, the government's primary responsibility to establish laws, maintain order and provide security, protect citizens from external threats, and promote the general welfare by providing public services.

None of those folks in those gas lines on the east coast in May would rate our response satisfactory.

While information sharing and cooperative investigative initiatives will not put an end to ransomware, they surely will enable some denting of the armor.

THE CONSTANT DRUMROLL

Attacks continue, and while everyone from Paxton Media Group to North Dakota's Sanford Health to Ibex, Vision for Hope, Chanel Korea, and the Durham Region Children's Health center reported incursions and successful breaches throughout the year, in lieu of revisiting each, it may be more useful to look at the emergence of a broader attack vector, that began to emerge in the first half, pulling ransomware apart.

The trend we see now is the open-source supply chain and the frightening part is it looks much bigger in terms of scope and scale and much more difficult to identify, defend, and stop in terms of complexity, depth, and reach.

DEPENDENCY CONFUSION

Most cybersecurity folks were hoping the International attention earlier attacks on Colonial and JBS received would have frightened the cyber-mob into hiding and re-organization, along with a resultant slowdown in the volume and nature of Ransomware.

Instead we saw a sidestep to these laboratory grade supply chain attacks against the open source ecosystem soar by 650% and a new vector class we call dependency confusion emerge, which is quickly becoming the over-reaching attack technique of choice to close out the year.

And indeed, the former eastern Euro gangs did take a momentary respite from savaging the Wild West. Our pesky friends at BlackMatter have just reemerged from DarkSide, the ransomware-as-a-service best known for the takedown of Colonial Pipeline.

Another gang whom we know as REvil had also been on staycation since their wildly successful attack on Kaseya, but we now see a completely refreshed online presence with new servers and a new list of victims.

None of these DarkWeb maneuvers matters, as what's important is the development of supply chain attacks against the open source ecosystem and it's soon to emerge dominance over all other attack vectors.

Some will call them sophisticated because instead of waiting for vulnerability disclosures, attackers are proactively injecting new vulnerabilities into open source projects that feed the global supply chain, and then exploiting the vulnerabilities they've created.

Sophisticated or otherwise, this form of cyber-attack will soon become the most deadly. And following the gangs is futile, becuase almost as soon as we recognize them by name, they dissolve and reconstitute as a new gang - like Conti did when it became Black Basta and hit 50 separate organizations during a 6 week window during April and May of this year.

HOUSTON, WE MAY HAVE A PROBLEM

I will spare you my rant on open-source in the most vulnerable attack landscapes, but the short-form version is "we have a problem."

Sonatype, a DevSecOps automation specialist, found that nearly three in 10 of the most popular Java, JavaScript, Python, and.NET projects contain at least one known security vulnerability. The challenge is that popular open-source projects have more known vulnerabilities overall, and developers using them are also less likely to be stuck in a situation where there is a known vulnerability but no remediation path.

But the reality implies that to stay in control and continue to support business initiatives, disciplined dev teams need to actively manage these dependencies and ensure they are moving to newer and non-vulnerable versions in a continuous manner.

Who does that?

Almost no one.

While development teams believe they are doing a good job fixing defective components and think they understand where risk resides, the empirical data tells a different story. In fact, the data says they make suboptimal decisions 69% of the time when updating third-party dependencies.

7 out of 10 is a stubborn fact.

Think about your own dev teams, then let's talk open-source some more.

Objectively, the research shows that most development teams are not following structured guidance with regard to dependency management and, as a result, they are not actively remediating known risk within their software supply chains.

Instead of waiting for OpenSSF or the Consortium for Information and Software Quality, I would stand up my own quality check and SBM initiative to prove that our internal team was working with maximized cleanliness and hygiene from the start.

THE PIVOTAL QUESTION

The pivotal question is does the rush to digitization and the fourth Industrial Revolution justify the exposure and vulnerability, and the expanded threat landscape we are bringing upon ourselves?

Process automation seems like a logical choice, yet when we consider GitHub's recently identified high-severity vulnerabilities in Node.js packages alone, which could be easily exploited to achieve arbitrary code execution, we realize we are expanding complexity rather than reducing it, and as we assess success with SOAR, are we convinced we have the level of automated intelligence equal to the task?

The last nine months have revealed several high-profile software supply chain attacks, including the SolarWinds hack that affected several U.S. government agencies, Microsoft, and FireEye, among other organizations, and the ransomware attack that encrypted the data of more than 1000 Kaseya VSA customers.

Those are also stubborn facts.

Instead of making progress against the growing tide of incoming cyber-attacks, it seems we set the table each month with new vulnerabilities and easier access paths, in effect, joining forces with our adversaries by easing access to our crown jewels. These efforts also get almost no media coverage either, seemingly in the same bucket as other International events that can't be easily explained and as a result, many in our industry wake up surprised at the increase in access points created almost magically overnight.

Is it that we cannot admit, acknowledge and accept that we are not up to do the required foundational hygienic work required in cybersecurity, or is it that we lack the leadership smarts to recognize that not all organizations are prepared for agile development and DevSecOps deployment, and that we also fail to recognize the dangers?

If we continue along the trail we have forged in 2021, our near-term destiny will continue to be earmarked by battlefield failure, most of which will be self-inflicted.

THE RISK THRESHOLD

To illustrate the threat and risk threshold, consider the state of today's open source supply, demand, and security dynamics:

> Supply has increased by 20% YOY. The top four open source ecosystems now contain a combined 37,451,682 different versions of components. You read that right.

Demand has followed and increased by 73% YOY. In 2021, it is estimated that global developers will download more than 2.2 *trillion* open source packages from the top four ecosystems. Despite the growing volume of downloads, the percentage of available components utilized in production applications is shockingly low.

We found projects with a faster mean time to update (MTTU) to be more secured, yet by a tiny factor of only 1.8 times less likely to contain vulnerabilities. We also saw that popularity is not a good predictor of security.

The most popular open source projects were 3X times more likely to contain vulnerabilities.

HOW THE OPEN SOURCE SUPPLY CHAIN OPERATES

A digital supply chain attack's objective is to infiltrate and disrupt the computer systems of a company's supply chain in order to harm that target company.

The premise is that key suppliers or vendors of a company may be more vulnerable to attack than the primary target, making them weak links in the target's overall network.

For example, the Target attack through their third-party vendor providing heating and air conditioning service company, Fazio Mechanical Services, carelessly allowed the bad guys to steal their network credentials and thus obtain admin access to the Target ERP system.

Small company, weak security systems, and lack of awareness.

Big, explosive result.

Supply chain attacks expose a conundrum in a company's supply network which discloses that an organization's cyber security controls are only as strong as that of the weakest party on the chain. Because of its development process, open source has a chain of contributors and dependencies before it ultimately reaches its end users. It is important that those responsible for their user or organization's security are able to understand and verify the security of this dependency supply chain, yet therein lies the rub.

Almost all companies dependent on open-source supply chain do not audit nor do they understand the exposures and vulnerabilities inherent in the software.

In an attempt to reverse the cycle and shore up the unknowns from the knowns, OpenSSF, a cross-industry collaboration that brings together technology leaders to improve the security of OSS is creating a future where participants in the open source ecosystem use and share high quality software, with security handled proactively, by default, and as a matter of course.

Unfortunately, its work to date on the problem has demonstrated no impactful progress of note.

Another organization working to address the challenge is the Consortium for Information and Software Quality, a special interest group under the technology standards body Object Management Group. One of the standards the organization is working on is the software equivalent of a bill of materials, for example. It will let enterprise customers know the components that go into the software they're using, and if any of those components have known security problems.

Microsoft is involved, as is the Linux Foundation and other big players, about 30 companies total.

Valiant effort, but if you are in the field with supply chain relationships, you will have to do your own work.

REFRESH

So, open-source is a reminder that any company that produces software or hardware for other organizations is a potential target of attackers because most of their product is drawn from open-source code and/or API repositories which may or may not be safe, nor dependednt upon other open source modules residing in some library waiting to be called with the same considerations later or in compile mode. Nation-state actors have deep resources and the skills to penetrate even the most security-conscious firms.

Security vendors can be juicy targets. In the case of SolarWinds, for example, one of the higher-profile companies breached was FireEye, a cybersecurity vendor. FireEye says that the attackers didn't get into customer-facing systems, just the penetration tools used for security testing. Mimecast, Microsoft and Malware Bytes, quickly joined that list.

The fact that any of these got hit at all is worrisome.

They demonstrate that any vendor is vulnerable and could be compromised. In fact, this fall, security vendor Immuniweb reported that 97% of the world's top 400 cybersecurity companies had data leaks or other security incidents exposed on the dark web, and 91 companies had exploitable website security vulnerabilities.

But this new focus on open-source is the most worrisome of all.

Today, the proliferation of open source vulnerabilities make it impossibly irresistible. In addition to the JPD (just plain dumb) threat, folks like China have been compromising U.S. military, government and critical civilian platforms for years so that intentionally folding a Chinese supplier into our supply chains is essentially suicidal, we continue.

In spite of that, nearly every government organization and private company is exposed, to some degree, to technology that originates in China or other low-cost supplier countries.

WHAT CAN WE DO?

If we are still committed to plowing ahead with business-driven digitalization initiatives, there are a few things that we can turn to for some level of support. Regulatory frameworks, in the financial sector or healthcare, already provide for third-party risk testing, or have some standards that vendors need to comply with, as within PCI, there's a software quality component to test the quality of mobile payment components.

The Capability Maturity Model (CMM), ISO 9001, Common Criteria, SOC 2, and FIPS-140, all of which should become part of audit criteria, regardless of cost and inconvenience.

If we start demanding more testing, or regulators step in and mandate better controls, then the costs of these audits are likely to drop and we will also see more innovation, such as bringing us back to the beginning in automated testing and orchestration.

We actually have effective AI/ML technologies that could take over these processes, but it may be that we are moving so fast, potential solution vendors are not even seeing the opportunities therein.

In our upcoming launch of CyberEd.io, we have dedicated a lot of heavy lifting to the issues around DevSecOps and open-source supply chain exposures, and it is our intent to keep the spotlight focused on this threat vector until we close the gap between the traps and the designs.

It can be done.

At Levi Strauss for example, the company vets its software vendors today by requiring them to have demonstrable, auditable proof that they have implemented a security framework and can demonstrate compliance with that framework, while taking a dim view of leveraging open source supply chain options.

It is all a function of your risk appetite and understanding your capabilities in context. JPMC will have a different view of each than a Levi Strauss.

Software works the way it works.

There is no Galaxy, where on Mars, software works one way and on Venus, it works another. This should represent a huge advantage to folks trying to defend against incoming, but the problem is in the ecosystem, the complexity, and the way it's put together.

We are enthusiastic proponents of Zero Trust and firmly believe that an organized campaign that starts with the identification of critical assets and the establishment of a small protect surface around those assets through network microsegmentation and rigorous least privilege with continual MFA, while limiting Internet facing software to minimal web access permissions is the pathway toward resetting our existing network environments within that Zero Trust context over time.

Many attack simulation experiments in the space have proven a 50% improvement in breach prevention, just from executing those few design principles, and it caused no one to rip and replace anything.

In today's tool and software markets, we have all of the required technology, so there is literally no acceptable excuse for anyone on the prosumer side to ignore Zero Trust principles and continue doing it as we have.

Whatever we do, it needs to be different than what we have done, or we will have no chance against these adversaries.

THE TARGET EXPANDS

Cyber-physical systems (CPSs) remain in the news (Colonial and JBS) as the vulnerabilities continue to surface while essentially becoming unmanageable in a cyber-threat context.

They are the heart-beat of all connected devices where security spans both the cyber and physical worlds, and combined with open-source supply chain threats will soon become world-shaking targets of attacks.

The open source TCP/IP stacks which are used to manage most of these devices, continue to expose hundreds of vendors and millions of their products in healthcare, manufacturing, pharmaceuticals, and critical infrastructure across energy, electrical, oil & gas and water systems and other lesser segments during 2021.

Internet of Medical Things (IoMT) brings this concept into hyper-focus where it is easy to imagine pacemakers and defibrillators being attacked and their users and/or providers held for hostage.

And dying.

Attacks targeting IoMT and health information technology generally continue to grow and vulnerabilities related to the pandemic are amplifying the threat. At the same time, health systems have been rapidly growing their device inventory to meet the insistence upon digitization, and the sudden surge in health care demands from COVID-19 while providing lifesaving treatment to those patients at grave risk.

And we now know that COVID-19 is one variant of many and that isolation, masking and vaccination may become our new realties, [or they may not].

Typically, because of the spinning pandemic clock, new IoMT, like those telehealth platforms, did not undergo more than a cursory security onboarding. The result is an expanded and significant risk to patient safety, personal health information (PHI) confidentiality, and the overall clinical network. Gartner predicts that the financial impact of CPS attacks resulting in fatal casualties will reach over $50 billion by 2023.

With OT, smart buildings, smart cities, connected cars and autonomous vehicles evolving, a focus on operational resilience needs an infusion of urgency.

CISA and the FBI have already increased the details provided around threats to critical infrastructure-related systems.

Now, CEOs will no longer be able to plead ignorance or hide behind insurance policies.

Gartner predicts that by 2024, liability for cyber-physical security incidents will begin to pierce the corporate veil for CEO protection and hold CEOs and other C-suite leaders and Board members accountable.

And with this shift in liability laws, we may actually make some progress in getting to proper levels of cybersecurity defense and preparedness.

After a few disasters and massive wrongful death lawsuits, the C-suite may finally come to realize that this "security business" is actually their first priority.

THE GOVERNMENT ACTS

The follow-on momentum from Biden's executive order (EO) signed in May, which outlines several cybersecurity measures and requirements intended to harden our nation's digital infrastructure will impact our world in several significant ways.

One, is a real timeline towards Federal agencies adopting Zero Trust architecture.

Most security protocols assume that if you have the credentials to access a certain network, you can be trusted to work in it. Zero Trust removes that assumption with continual multi-factor authentication and more expansive data encryption, microsegmentation, protect surfaces and a focus on data, access, applications and services.

Within 60, 90, and 180 days of the order being issued, agencies will be required to first, update their existing plans to adopt Zero Trust cloud technology and second to work with the Department of Homeland Security (DHS) and the General Services Administration (GSA) to develop and issue cloud-based security standards.

While the order addresses seven core areas, sections on software supply chain security and threat information sharing requirements within one year, are most likely to have an impact on businesses.

Organizations may not realize they are bound by the order – even if they aren't a federal contractor.

And finally, the requirement to actually adopt and implement the Zero Trust architecture described earlier.

The SBOM (Software Bill of Materials) is in there, and while it would not have helped in the SolarWinds fiasco, it will help our DevSecOps teams better prepare for open-source, supply chain attacks. Similar to FDA requirements for medical devices such as pacemakers, SBOM requirements are expected to require that organizations list all the components used in their software, including libraries, drivers, firmware, licenses, and operating systems. The order also requires that organizations secure their software development processes and access controls.

To Whom Will it Apply?

Essentially everyone, as your software development company is likely to be part of the federal government software supply chain even if you don't know it. By extension, any vendors whose products are used by those developers—hardware providers, for example—are part of the chain.

Besides direct federal contractors, the order also applies to broad commercial subsectors. Companies that supply to defense contractors (or whose software or hardware end up in a contractor's products or services) are in the supply chain and in a position to introduce risk.

Additionally, it is expected that the National Institute of Standards and Technology (NIST) will publish supply chain security standards that will likely become a security industry standard. Software and hardware suppliers to state and local government and private sector should expect changes to become compliance requirements in the future.

LATE ENTRIES

Looking back on the supply chain attack on NEW Coop, the farmer's feed and grain cooperative with over sixty locations throughout Iowa, we are impressed with the extent of technology and planninng that combined to pull that one off.

Demonstrating just how deeply and broadly the U.S. economy and our supply chains are interconnected, our BlackMatter friends dealt a ransomware attack to this network that supplies 40% of U.S. grain production and 11 million animals' feed schedules, demanding $5.9 million in exchange for not leaking stolen data and a decryptor.

What was seized included 1000 gigabytes worth of files, including invoices, research, and development documents, and the source code to its soil-mapping technology.

The ransom request will increase to $11.8 million if a not paid within five days.

BlackMatter, as you may recall, was one of the gangs who promised they would not target "Critical infrastructure facilities (nuclear power plants, power plants, water treatment facilities)."

Now with $12 million hanging in the balance, NEW Coop begged BlackMatter for an explanation, given that they think of themselves as critical infrastructure, and that the attack will lead to food supply disruption for grain, pork, and chicken.

NEW went further to plead with BlackMatter, "I am just telling you this so you are not surprised as it does not seem like you understood who we are and what role our company plays in the food supply chain."

This one is worth watching as it can potentially set the direction for a bunch of different weather vanes.

A TEXTBOOK CLASSIC FOR THE FUTURE

One last breach just discovered in the closing moments of 2021 deserves mention however, in that it is a living example of the absence of hygiene, and due care and the broadening target value.

D.W. Morgan, a multinational supply chain management and logistics company based in the United States, left an Amazon S3 bucket open without authorization controls, exposing sensitive data relating to shipments and the company's clients.

As the market leader, D.W. Morgan, a $240 million logistics company provides services to some of the biggest companies in the world and all of their data, including IP is lying exposed on the Internet. It is the exact same breach that cost Cap-1 over a hundred million USD two years ago. In this case, more than 2.5 million files were exposed containing transportation plans and agreements outlining every step of the shipment process for each exposed D.W. Morgan client, including huge companies like Cisco and Ericsson.

That data represents shipping instructions, and full PII for every Morgan employee, client employee, and ship to employee involved in each transaction.

Which opens the doors to a myriad of scams and fraud, but in particular, cybercriminals could contact client businesses and their employees, referencing shipment details to build trust. From here, hackers could target employees and client businesses with various scams, like the fake invoice scheme.

With invoice details, bad guys will have no trouble convincing harrowed WFH employees that extra charges or half or all of the invoice value must be paid prior to completion of the shipment. Since client employees had their full names and contact details exposed, the attackers could call or message, referencing details of shipments (like prices or goods ordered) to masquerade as a colleague, D.W. Morgan employee, or a representative of a supplier. Once the client employee trusts the hacker, the attacker could also convince them to click on a malicious link.

D.W. Morgan's third-party suppliers have had their details exposed, too, which means hackers can expand their phishing to many additional organizations. What is inside an attack is not always obvious to the industry observer and some of these repercussions will manifest themselves later as they emerge from the long tail following this primary attack.

This swarm effect will continue throughout 2022 and beyond as complexity expands, hygiene suffers, APIs dominate, open-source continues to carry the programming load, more data and processing is pushed to the hybrid cloud, and fewer companies will be able to cope with an overwhelming enemy force.

Having said that, we don't like predictions.

They are either too Captain Obvious and safe to make, or too fanciful to imagine properly. But it would be fair to find out what our expectations, based on our research for next year might look like.

PREDICTIONS

So, here's our top-ten list:

1. Physical infrastructure will top the list of dangerous attacks with serious outcomes.

   We need to accelerate our Operational Technology defenses. That will mean closing entire factories and plants for days at a time, but it must be done. We don't for the most part lack the tools, skills, or detection capabilities to prevent OT attacks. What we lack is the organized, pro-active will to launch a unified SCADA and ICS-wide protection campaign. We anticipate with 50% confidence that following the next physical attack on critical infrastructure, a community group will form who can force companies to pause production for as long as it takes to get a solid cyber-defense plan in place and implement it.

2. Double-extortion Ransomware attacks like the one imposed on Shutterfly will continue.

   This is a no brainer for the prognosticators as this form of Ransomware attack has proven so successful. A double-extortion attack first steal's a company's data, and then threatens to publish it on the web to ratchet up the pressure to pay a ransom. It works. In fact, over 16 ransomware groups actively utilize this tactic.

By mid-2020, hundreds of organizations became double ex-tortion victims, dark net websites began leaking company data, and the Ransomware-as-a-Service (RaaS) business model took off as developers were able to sell and rent new malware strains.

As, cyber security regulations started advertising their fines for violations, cyber-criminals began weaponizing the compliance fines (CCPA, GDPR, NYSDFS) to push their victims by offering them a ransom smaller than the penalty fee, in exchange for their quiescence.

In addition, because there is so much more to lose from double extortion ransomware, companies will do well to spend as many focused calories as possible on overcoming the threat. Zero Trust is a great place to start that journey. No matter what is paid for a transition to a Zero Trust strategy, it will be a pittance compared with the cost of mitigating a Ransomware attack, especially one of the double extortion variety.

3. Open-source supply-chain attacks will continue to grow with no solution in sight.

The problem with open-source supply-chain attacks is the one that SecDef Rumsfeld referred to when he now famously pointed out that, "Reports that say that something hasn't happened are always interesting to me, because as we know, there are known knowns; there are things we know we know. We also know there are known unknowns; that is to say we know there are some things we do not know. But there are also unknown unknowns—the ones we don't know we don't know. And if one looks throughout the history of our country and other free countries, it is the latter ca-tegory that tends to be the difficult ones."

Open-source carries the freight of unknown unknown de-pendencies on other open-source code that is difficult and sometimes impossible to identify. Not only are we under-resourced to examine the selected code we extract from open-source libraries to become part of our next software release, we never conduct extended investigation into what these modules will call in the wild.

It is the equivalent to sending a train down the tracks without any controls, including brakes.

How bad is it?

Whoo-hoo bad.

According to Sonatype's annual State of the Software Supply Chain Report, these attacks numbered more than 12,000 – a 650% increase over 2020, following a 430% increase over 2019.

The report also named "Dependency confusion" attacks as the most common form.

This class of attack has the bad guys proactively injecting new vulnerabilities into open source that feeds the global supply chain, and then exploiting the brand new (to our defense technologies) vulnerabilities they've created.

While development teams seem to be doing a good job fixing defective components and apparently demonstrating an understanding of resident risk, the Sonatype data tells a different story. In fact, the report says they make suboptimal decisions 69% of the time when updating third-party dependencies.

According to the report findings, "the research shows that most development teams are not following structured guidance with regard to dependency management and, as a result, they are not actively remediating known risk within their software supply chains."

And that alone is enough for bad guys to continue attacking these gold mines of compromise opportunity.

Intelligent automation may appear to hold an answer, and it is estimated that a medium-sized enterprise with 20 application development teams would save a total of 160 developer days a year, representing hundreds of thousands of dollars.

But, our own research can't find any examples where companies are leveraging automation within the DevSecOps function, thus failing to address the overall risk factors driving the threat landscape.

Unless a solution is found and uniformly adapted, we will continue to see expanding attacks on open-source supply chains with newly discovered accelerants being used to blow up the curve.

4. Folks will continue to accelerate the use of open-source database management systems.

In spite of the rise in open-source database management systems attacks, popular open source databases (MySQL, PostgreSQL and MongoDB, etc.) have seen increased adoption by as many as 53% by enterprises. On paper, the attraction is straightforward and compelling: cost savings, ease of use, the avoidance of vendor lock-in, and community editions are the main reasons for the popularity. OSS is also of course, generally believed to be more secure because more eyes are fixing discovered problems and playing watchdog for new vulnerabilities.

In the real-world however, the known security issues with OSS need in-depth expertize and very few developers are security experts. Those who are, do not have time to walk the beat.

Some of the most common threats lying within open-source database management systems include.

Excessive privileges: same as proprietary DBMS's and should be addressed through robust and granular identity access management systems.

Privilege abuse: Users may misuse privileges but as is the case in their real-life brethren, most Open Source DBMS's lack the appropriate access control policies to mitigate and the senior C-suite seems to always enjoy complete and unfettered access whether they need it or not.

Unauthorized privilege escalation: Attackers who seize administrative privileges are easily able to may convert low-level access to high-level privileges. Without behavioral analytics built into policy engines, we can never achieve appropriate levels of confidence necessary to apprehend and block these access requests.

Every one of these access and authorization threats can be overcome through a Zero Trust implementation program.

Most open source databases have security issues around access controls and secure communication, enough so that project teams should avoid them at all costs. In addition, security tools are almost always absent. Third party vendors do not publish their formalized internal assessment results, or identify their monitoring, auditing or masking tools because the demand doesn't justify the costs.

That statement alone explains most of what is wrong with the current direction.

Until companies stop using open-source database management system in lieu of proprietary DBMs from the industry leaders, we will continue to present opportunities by the bushel-full to every attacker roaming the web. False economies driven by developer ego, or something else?

5. As Web App attacks sky-rocket, we will see a rush to protect APIs.

Another open-source dilemma in that many and sometimes all of the APIs we use come from open-source repositories. We get that, but since it is a major source of easy entry points for bad guys, it seems to us that we should shut them down in a unified show of force and keep them shut down until we figure out how to accommodate their inclusion in our code.

The security risks of open APIs are not just limited to hackers as general use can lead to data sharing among many different applications. APIs need the same level of identity authentication and proofing as all other services, perhaps an even greater focus could be argued as APIs generally collect wide swaths of user data as they march toward their functionality.

Right now, we do none of that identity management at the API level and since we don't monitor either, we have no idea how deep and wide the vulnerability is and what we need to do to offset the damage.

Preventing the damage is another conversation and there we have two choices. We can stop using open-source APIs altogether, or we can adopt a Zero Trust strategy and framework that will lead us to policy shifts appropriate for any component of DAAS, including API access of any kind.

Our prediction?

Business as usual and dramatic increases in open API-related compromise.

6. Active Directory will continue to dominate as the world's most powerful Trojan.

Back before the Internet, the business world was supported by a series of small directories that made sharing key data and files a possibility, yet required a lot of painful effort to make work. Users would have to log into each file system, and provide a set of credentials and applications required for access. Since that quickly became thousands of file systems, change was needed.

Along came Windows NT and Microsoft had already been helping companies to adopt domains, which enabled the joining of multiple systems within a circle of "trust."

The effect reduced the segmentation of user identities into various different directories, all managed by a function known as AD or Active Directory.

However, the scalability limitations of Windows NT domains meant that multiple domain directories needed to be built and managed in different geographies with trusts between them, which became increasingly challenging as both businesses and systems behind them were joining the globalization and digital transformation movement.

Most troubling is the fact that while Microsoft introduced a flawed Active Directory (AD) as a solution to that problem, creating bigger problems along the way, yet even today, remains the leader in remote computing support.

Introduced as an open system, AD users merely had to demonstrate they were logged into their system with a legitimate AD account.

My, has the world changed.

This openness, while applauded as a positive game changer at the turn of the century, has now been proven to be AD's most glaring vulnerability and provides anyone with the flimsiest of verified credentials complete administrative access everywhere on the network. In fact, AD remains a strong and unquestioned foundational piece of infrastructure for 90% of businesses. Most business applications today don't bother with a proprietary directory, opting instead on their users to be proven Windows authenticated.

The fact that this is not a surprise to anyone working in the field for a few years, is part of the psychological puzzle that keeps us chasing our tails – which we address and explain in subsequent chapters.

We are spending a big chunk of time on this topic here, because its native connectedness is far more compelling and far-reaching than any other easily compromised systems tool, that even if we achieve 20% of what we seek, it won't be without further corruption at the OS level.

More and more attack vectors continue to be found and documented publicly, thus creating a road map for cybercriminals to use.

And use it, they do – in fact, most Ransomware attacks originate with AD.

A good example can be found in AD's service principal names (SPN), which is the way that a Kerberos client uniquely identifies an instance of a service for a given Kerberos target computer.

Due to AD's openness, a bad guy is easily able to find privileged SPNs in any computing environment and by combining those with domain admin accounts, can easily create maximum privileges and complete visibility.

Once inside the network, the bad guys will leverage AD to find your critical assets, extract them, encrypt them and then demand a double-extortion ransom payment. And despite all of the thought leadership around these topics over the years, most businesses are not prepared.

The impact of continued preparation failure will lead to an increasingly vicious cycle of attack, collect, encrypt, notify, demand, monetize, realize and move on to the next victim.

The path is clear to create a hardened environment, likely impervious to serious Ransomware damages, yet those roadmaps continue to be ignored as more and more companies find themselves stuck in the lower gears and forced to pay the ransom.

As you can see, there are several things we can do to put an end to this threat. They start with a Zero Trust strategy and end with rip and replace, education and strong offensive security.

If we were to bet on winners in the coming years, our money is on the bad guys.

7. Microsoft Windows and O365 will remain the most vulnerable and porous targets for attackers.

IBM's Cost of a Data Breach Report 2021, tells us that the average cost of a data breach in 2021 alone increased by the largest year-over-year margin of the last seven years combined. In 2020, the cost was $3.86M. In 2021 it climbed to $4.24M.

In addition, the average time elapsed before breach detection in 2021 was 212 days requiring an additional 75 days to contain it! Both of those numbers are higher than any in history.

Microsoft vulnerabilities that lead to compromised domains and criminals creating their own accounts with full admin credentials were responsible for 20% of 2021 breaches and resulted in an average cost of $4.37M per breach.

Consider this: Over 1 million companies' globally and over 731,000 companies in the United States that use Office 365. Adding to this obvious attack environment, there are 100,000 Microsoft partners facilitating services and products for clients. It should then surprise no one that vulnerabilities in Microsoft products present a highly popular set of attack targets.

Why we insist on using porous and vulnerable products as the backbone for our global computing eco-system is a really good question that we try to answer in subsequent chapters.

In the meantime, we know that the most critical Microsoft vulnerabilities lie within five categories that are used frequently. By everyone. They include Exchange vulnerabilities, Print Spooler vulnerabilities, Sensitive Windows Registry database files vulnerabilities, Encrypting File System Remote Protocol (MS-EFSRPC) and Active Directory Certificate Services (AD CS) vulnerabilities, and ActiveX vulnerabilities.

Exchange vulnerabilities complicate Microsoft's Exchange Server, which is the most widely used and well-known email platform for global governments and business enterprises.

Not unlike most everything we deal with today, managing the Exchange Server in-house is a complex task, and our frequent misconfiguration and patching mistakes make up a target rich environment for threat actors looking to exploit vulnerable Exchange servers based on configuration and patching scan results.

Recent Microsoft Exchange Server vulnerabilities include ProxyLogon, which exploits the Exchange Proxy Architecture and its Logon mechanism, allowing bad guys to bypass authentication, impersonate an administrator and gain code execution abilities across the entire network.

Print Spooler vulnerabilities let bad guys with low-privilege domain user accounts take control of a server running on the Print Spooler service and add dynamic link library (DLL) files as printer drivers. We do a lot of printing. Once the vulnerability is exploited, bad actors are free to install programs, mess with data, and create new users with full permissions anywhere on network.

I could go, but I am thinking you get the point by now.

But just in case, there are also default Windows 10 and 11 configurations that grant all non-admin users read rights on key registry hives.

What?

Yes. It is a known error.

By accessing and retrieving all Registry hives within Windows, cyber-crooks can use SAM (Security Account Manager) data to execute their own code and create authentication for their machine instance. This provides full control enabling any commands, any payload drops, and the ability to create endless, fully-permissioned users.

Nope. Not making any of this up.

If you were of recent Martian descent, you would likely be asking why we continue to rely on this single, 160 million lines of code Frankensteinying version of the core business OS backbone upon which we then build tens of millions of applications, systems and network dependencies that are somehow the digital infrastructure of our future.

We don't know why we do that but, to the issue of whether or not there are any signs that this condition will improve in the next five years?

The answer is, no.

8. Complexity will continue to increase, exacerbated by hybrid cloud storage, APIs and 5G.

Start with 5G, which among all three impact players, has the simplest problem profile. 5G is faster than 4G with more bits-per-second able to travel the network.

The most noticeable impact for most is the speed differential in movie downloads under 5G – try seconds versus minutes.

5G is lower latency, and brings data and updates into users and systems much more quickly.

5G requires less power and can rapidly switch to low-energy use when cellular radios are not in use.

5G uses bandwidth more effectively and relies on many more connection points. This will reduce network costs by removing stress and all costs overall should improve.

5G, allowed to leverage more radio waves than 4G, should enable more devices and less congestion.

Having said all that, 5G is wrought with challenges:

5G requires more transmitters to cover the same area as current 4G networks. Replacement cells are challenging as protected historical sites or rough geography prevent easy rip and replace approaches.

5G cybersecurity needs some significant improvements, including decentralized security like that found at Target, Whole Foods, or Walmart. Pre-5G networks had fewer hardware traffic points, which made it relatively easy to do security checks and maintenance, but someone should tell 5G producers that dynamic software-based systems have far more traffic routing points, and thus present many more single points of failure, all of which need to be monitored.

None of this is in place now or moving in that direction, so we will see many more captured unsecured real estate and the rapid compromise of other parts of the network.

More bandwidth will challenge real-time threat monitoring and put a hard burden on current security monitoring, including older networks that are limited in speed and capacity, and thus enable real-time monitoring which has helped with detection and discovery and particularly in systems based in behavioral science.

100X new speeds net out to a sizable increase in the burden to provide new methods for stopping threats that find benefit is speedier delivery.

IoT, IIoT and IoMD devices are consciously manufactured without addressing security or at the very least the awareness of the need for multiple versions to suit the security regulations of multiple states. Most of these devices rely on small margins and large volumes in order to remain successful in these challenging times.

Devices made in Nevada and shipped to the Southeast for sale, will not address each state's security legislation and opt for a one-size fits all approach that will likely supersede the inspecting agency – the theory being that it is easier and less costly to beg forgiveness, than to ask permission, riding on the belief that the odds against inspection are strong.

As we have argued throughout, lots of intelligence assist folks in rapid discovery whatever color hat they might wear.

As more devices connect, billions of devices with non-standard security attention translates to billions of future breach points. Any connected device, no matter how small or stupid, provides a network point of weakness. Today's enormous vacuum of security standards in the entire IoT space, including SCADA and ICS systems will continue to lead to increased breaches and complicated attacks.

Again, we can anticipate your questions, yet we have no answers.

There have been numerous attempts at creating standards by NIST and other governing bodies, but adoption still depends upon Federal mandates and/or individual manufacturers voluntary compliance with state-level security requirements.

Outlook: Dim.

The extra attention required by 5G security will require that Network operators and providers begin collaborating with cybersecurity firms to develop advanced encryption solutions, network monitoring approaches, and new, speed-adjusted detection and remediation techniques that lean heavily on Ai and ML.

We are nowhere near those capabilities today.

Consumer education on IoT cybersecurity should become one necessary component of larger eLearning initiatives which need to be designed with a consumer-centric voice and cover a range of topics all designed for retention and comprehension. The goal would be to provide an understanding of each device's approach to security and the supply-chain affect or domino impact of a single device compromised along the way.

We all now live in a digital age and none of us will be able to escape the requirement for security fundamentals that should be within the cornerstone of consumer use.

Does it exist today? No.

One approach to smoothing that adoption is through a labeling system similar to that used by the FDA, directed at safely levels and warnings for every connected IoT device. In addition, the FCC provides a grading system for radio transmissions that could easily find a good use-case home in the consumer sector.

Adding to the slope of adoption, efforts to improve security have yet to translate into real-world results, and is an indication of the long path yet to be traveled alongside the 5G rollout.

We anticipate a long, long tail of security corrections, modifications and patches as we enable this rollout which may appear to the casual observer, similar in nature to that we are engineering alongside our O365 adoption which began years ago and is still fraught with many active and critical vulnerabilities.

Cloud security is an "all-in" raise on top of our enterprise 5G bet.

The primary danger in implementing simple cloud security and dimensional hybrid cloud solutions is complexity. Anytime one adds another element to their network topology, one must make a conscious risk decision after first quantifying the extent of damages associated with a complexity-centric breach alongside the probability of that event occurring.

We can tell you now that the probability is high and it grows higher when implemented amid a 5G environment.

An incremental move, while best, requires decisions around application splits, a frank assessment of one's internal capabilities and ability to deal with cloud-related security compliance requirements.

If as a healthcare provider, for example, you are required to continuously encrypt all patient data at every stage, a lack of encryption capability on your cloud provider's behalf could interrupt your migration plans and place the burden back on you to develop cloud encryption while the data resides at rest in your local cloud.

Maybe you don't split that application, but your network traffic might need to be encrypted, and/or you may face unique regulatory standards for search and data archiving requirements that are part of your state's legislative oversight.

And maybe, while your intentions are good and you have invested all of the blood, sweat and years to be ready for this conversion, you find it impossible to recruit and hire the kind of talent that can manage a transition like this.

We think that scenarios like the one just described add a subtle layer of complexity onto an already sensitive threat profile made even more delicate by the imposition of cloud storage and 5G.

Adding insult to injury, we also have now opened the gates to a global threat as the cloud provides that access through the ubiquitous nature of the global cloud and our inability to manage it.

Because you need to be sure you have provided strong authentication granularity for all of your hybrid cloud resources through multi-factor identification. If you lack that knowledge and skilled resources to manage the implementation and policy engines, you will not be able to leverage the cloud in any easy way.

Bottom line if you have the authority: Stay away from cloud or hybrid cloud implementations until the space is proven to be natively secure.

With your "all-in" bet now called by the dark web, your choices are limited. Since you can't lose any more than you have already bet, you may as well lay your reputation on the table and throw in some APIs.

The Open Web Application Security Project (OWASP) is a trusted nonprofit foundation that publishes software security analysis and is well-known for its yearly roundup of top web application vulnerabilities. It is the trusted repository that continually identifies those APIs that are vulnerable and the specific vulnerabilities they carry along with any known fixes that may be applied to Band-Aid the vulnerability.

The repository is an open invite for security gatekeepers to find the exact exploits that these APIs thrive upon and provide the methods for patching the holes.

As we see the utility of these APIs increase, they become more vulnerable to attack, but if we dedicate resources, use the OWASP repository and leverage our hygiene skills, we see that a safe path forward lies in a few simple security strategies, all based on the Zero Trust principles:

Since APIs enable access to lots of services, data, and applications, if authorization is ever broken, we see an instant expansion of the attack surface. Thus, the key to API security is to make sure we have authorization to API-accessible objects locked down and that we an API gateway to assure most of the authorization is bulletproof.

There are at least a dozen or more best practices that are strongly recommended to protect against rogue APIs. But none exist for open source APIs which are where the real danger lies. We use open source APIs because they are easily available, cut significant time off our development schedules and appear to be secure. We never have the resources to check on that security or to vet either the source or the dependencies the APIs call once activated in the wild.

So, no matter how you slice it, by using open-source APIs we are inviting unknown terrorists onto our networks and into our data. And we should put an end to this practice.

But entering this fray at any time will surely put you into an impossible security situation that will be exacerbated by all of the fundamental issues like patching and general configuration hygiene that have yet to be adequately addressed throughout industry.

Our recommendation would be to stay clear of both cloud and 5G until we see some wrinkle free surfaces to assure us that cybersecurity progress is being made. And never use open-source APIs under any circumstances

9. The skills gap will widen even more dramatically than in the past. Why?

Because in spite of the 70 plus players in the online eLearning space, no one has put together a curriculum based on what CISOs need from the perspective of the CISOs themselves.

Can you find Python programming courses, certification test preparation for a CRISC badge and cyber range training for attack simulations? Of course you can.

Are they embedded within a context and structured as a part of a holistic program designed to teach the skills that are in the highest demand across a set of unified global training requirements? They are not.

In addition, no one has been willing to allocate resources to each enterprise license to assure that value is extracted. Not dissimilar to complex enterprise software licenses, the result has been that training courses sit on digital shelves long after the first wave of training is administered. This latency shows up most dangerously in security awareness training where what we needed to know last month has morphed into something new this month.

Our mission at CyberEd.io is to develop the most productive, efficient and easy-to-use online eLearning cybersecurity training available in any market and roll it out through our subscriber network of over 1 million senior security practitioners, CISOs and cyber-warriors, spread across every industry segment and global geolocation.

But in the meantime, we will continue to see a natural expansion as vulnerability exploits are packed into as-a-service offerings and sold for a combination of fees plus profit percentage to folks with almost no computer training while our defenders become less relevant to new threat vectors every week

10. The global geo-political stage will be dominated by cyber-attack scenarios in real-time

Geopolitics is the study of the geographical effects that politics and international relations has on world conditions and how actions, interactions, and relations between countries affect some major outcomes throughout history.

While typically and historically concerned with purely geographical dimensions, our continuous digitization and the world's increasing reliance on the Internet has developed cyberspace into a primary battlefield on which aggressive nation states can compete against other nation states and augment their more limited warfare capabilities in the physical world.

When compared to the cost of conventional armed forces and the ongoing expense of engagement in the real world, digital tools that can easily be leveraged by cyber-aggressors can potentially cause devastating outcomes for the targeted entities and can for a few dollars, be launched quickly and in near-real time, yet are able to create chaos and inflict severe business interruption for their consistency.

We have described in detail the threats inherent within the global battlefields related to nation-state actors and where the United States stands in regard to equivalent cyber-capabilities in 2022.

Just today, the Cybersecurity and Infrastructure Security Agency (CISA) released a joint advisory with the National Security Agency (NSA) and the FBI, warning that Russian threat actors are leveraging certain tactics, techniques and procedures to infiltrate critical infrastructure.

In the advisory, CISA lays out several measures to detect and mitigate threats posed by the state actors, with a particular focus on critical infrastructure.

"CISA, the FBI, and NSA encourage the cybersecurity community – especially critical infrastructure network defenders – to adopt a heightened state of awareness and to conduct proactive threat hunting," the advisory says. It encourages security teams to implement mitigation strategies immediately.

You will likely be reading about this or have read about the fallout from this by the time this book gets published and it is only one example of many that we could point to on a daily basis that lead to increased global threats.

The future is not bright.

The good news?

There are things we can do.

NATIONAL SERVICE

Because we all now live in a digital world and cannot continue to ignore our individual responsibilities to manage our digital environments with dutiful care, it has been recommended that, in addition to the earlier described solutions, a model for a National Cybersecurity Service (NCS) program be mandated as a two-year public service requirement for every college graduate in the country – a war-time peace corps – less than half the service requirement for graduates of Annapolis – and/or 18-year olds who want to pursue a career path in cybersecurity without attending college.

The Israeli's didn't manage to survive all these years by pretending their enemies were their trading partners. In much the same way as the Israeli Defense Forces (IDF) accommodates varying interests, our own NCS would offer different specialty educational opportunities, but the program concentration would be on a warrior-level and offensive cyber training.

Framed as a Manhattan project, such a program can be both authorized and funded by Presidential order (ala FDR) and Congressional mandate (though many would question whether any recent Congress would have either the political appetite or courage to do so). Regardless of cost, it would likely be dwarfed by legislation that we push through our law-making process on a daily basis and would be the only initiative aimed directly at a true existential threat, and one acting as a clear and present danger, and not just a measurable, abstract probability ten years into the future.

But if we don't do something really soon, it won't matter how many new technologies we invent, how much new cyber-threat awareness we create in our corporate boardrooms, or how many new initiatives we create around the traditional approaches to managing cybersecurity. If we don't shift our approach to a risk management model, re-build our cyber-defense infrastructure on the basis of a Zero Trust architecture, and staff it with an abundance of trained warriors, we will continue to retreat from this cyber-war front in the business of business, out-resourced, out-smarted, and out-intimidated by opposing forces unencumbered by layers of social justice and political correctness, just as we have been doing for the last 20 years.

And at a national security level, all of the submarines, aircraft carriers, jet fighters or other military hardware, and human resources we can muster against our enemies in some conventional theater of war, won't matter either.

CHAPTER 6

Advertising Our Vulnerabilities

I s it obvious that organizations with fewer references to cybersecurity in their annual reporting are less security mature and more likely to be breached? Or, is it more likely that cybersecurity is not high enough on the agenda for the board and executive to feature it in their flagship report?

With the annual report being such a significant communications tool, we can use it as an indicator as to the strength of the top-down security culture within an organization.

But so can our adversaries.

In a stunning example of this information asymmetry, we see that cyber-criminals can follow a similar process as part of their open-source intelligence, identifying likely corporate victims perceived as the lowest hanging fruit. It is not a coincidence that Marriot, Anthem, Equifax, Yahoo, Home Depot, Sony, Adobe, etc., were among the many with the fewest references to cybersecurity in their pre-breach 10Ks.

If we stay in denial and do nothing to change the course, in the next few years, the cybersecurity landscape will worsen significantly and any chance of protecting information assets, assuring truthful social media, and providing data privacy will disappear completely.

Existential threats? Forget about global warming. Years from now, we all may be speaking a different language.

DOI: 10.1201/9781003331773-7

REVERSE COURSE

How can we reverse the course and get ahead?

1. Change the reporting rules and prevent companies from reporting on their cyber-vulnerabilities;

2. Apply granular controls over all Chinese-owned venture capital firms, or just shut them down;

3. Stop using any products or services, including mobile devices and telecom made in China;

4. Develop and apply rigorous process for fundamental hygiene with consequences;

5. Start sharing in earnest between public and private sectors;

6. Modernize our cyber-laws to enable offensive security;

7. Mandate a Zero Trust migration for every computing environment within an aggressive time-frame;

8. Create and enforce national security mandates that specify technologies (not products) that must be part of every Zero Trust implementation;

9. Create the equivalent of a Manhattan project for the application of AI/ML to the problem space, with appropriate funding and speed to market; and

10. Implement mandates on insurance providers to match coverage against a standardized NIST framework requirement.

By removing excessive trust from our systems and networks, isolating our critical assets, amping the identity authentication process, and reducing the overall attack surface, we will have removed 50% of the breach risk, and made cyber-criminals jobs much harder.

By eliminating products and services provided by our number one adversary, we will put an end to pre-engineered leakage and the impossibility to detect hardware vulnerabilities.

By throwing the IP thieves out of our tents, we will stop the theft of the key technologies that our adversaries now use against us.

By re-engineering the way we apply fundamental hygiene for patch and configuration management, we can decrease the number of vulnerabilities we now present.

By modernizing cybersecurity laws, we will remove the handcuffs that currently hinder law enforcement from apprehension and prosecution. In addition, we can open the doorways to a controlled offensive or forward defensive cybersecurity program at the national level, so that targets and victims can identify and seize bad actors in the process of committing their crimes.

By establishing mandates (vs. recommended) national security rules, we will assure that every organization is building and managing their IT and OT systems in accord with best practices that have demonstrated their ability to increase resiliency while decreasing risk. One mandate can cover ransomware attacks, by preventing the payout, but also providing insured coverage for the damage recovery, adjusting for negligence, and attendant liability, within 60 days of the attack under the jurisdiction of a special court.

By insisting on a mutual sharing of information and intelligence, private industry will have access to signals and behavioral data, now protected, which will enrich new product design and development.

By instituting an aggressive AI/ML Manhattan project, we will be able to expand the concept of a YCombinator with a specific product focus, aggressive funding, curation and vetting, and guidance from experts in those disciplines. It took only four years and $2 billion ($40 billion in 2022 dollars) to produce FatMan from whole cloth – it should take half that time and twice the money today.

By forcing insurers to provide and align their coverage against a standard for proper defense and controls, the burden is transferred to NAIC and FIO, forcing an actuarial proxy that will mature over time, yet set consistent expectations for both insurers and insured.

If we do all of this, will cyber-crime come to an end? Will we reverse the asymmetry within our current attacker–defender dynamic? Will we achieve world peace?

Of course not, BUT … .

It will begin a reversal of course and shift momentum to our team.

One of our self-inflicted wounds, however, is not fought with cyber-criminals, nation-states, or our own security teams, resource gaps, training, patches, configurations, and general hygiene.

It is being fought instead in the swamps of marketing warfare, competing with each other for precious little CISO mindshare, and stumbling to adopt yesterday's techniques and gimmicks to today's audience. Some of the resulting frustration results in mis-representations, exaggerated competencies matching exaggerated threats, inauthentic messaging, and downright harassment of the targeted buyer, the CISO.

So, while we are looking at a restart across ten competitive fronts in the direct war, we should reconsider how we are trying to reach our own partners and future customers.

ALTERNATE MARKETING

From a marketing point of view, we believe we may be on the brink of change in the way our industry typically allocates budget and the focus our programs and campaigns have traditionally taken. Many cybersecurity vendors today are considering alternate approaches to marketing outreach, either through bespoke events or through media channels with video content, shot live and on location with cinematic scripts and narratives focused on stories and not on solutions or value.

Known as "Branded Content," these stories ignore your product or service and focus instead on your values, purpose, and reason, giving your audience an opportunity to embrace you and engage with you without the frontal pressure of aggressive ad campaigns that answer questions not asked with answers not believed.

That latter form of outreach comes as the recognition of capturing CISO attention is failing via conventional approaches to content like white-papers, eBooks, and solution briefs.

CISOs have no time for our messages and 17-page product explanations, and are under unprecedented pressure from zero-day disasters like Log4j. Now is not a good time to reach these folks.

And when we DO reach out, through which channels will we reach?

Why does every NFL broadcast combo include a former player or coach?

Because we trust folks who talk about various strategies and tactics, but only those folks who have been in the trenches long enough to truly understand the game, and by doing so, can lend "color" to the broadcast that informs and educates.

Tony Romo and Troy Aikman are examples of former players who offer play-by-play insights that add some value to our viewing time. The Manning brothers are examples of a formula that fails epically.

The latter is not, by the way, the fault of the Manning brothers. They are great at chatting aimlessly and finding comedy in the game of football. Some producer somewhere must have been ecstatic when the project was green-lighted. The only problem is they all forgot about the game and why viewers were tuning in.

There are some former and current CISOs and C-suite executives in cybersecurity companies who are terrific at adding color and who understand the role that must be played and type of content the audience craves.

They are story-tellers by nature and they surround themselves with a team who can keep them on their toes through the interview. The support includes a proper background, dress, lighting, grooming, and set styling.

Then, there are many others who go through the motions yet can't seem to connect with the audience.

Interestingly, there is often a 1:1 mapping between the leader's style and their website and messaging.

The things we ignore win the argument for preparation. The things we notice and that distract us from the content, underscore how important preparation is for an effective video.

If marketers approach this important medium without a fundamental understanding of what works and what doesn't, and/or without emphasis on the former, the poorly prepared speaker turns marketing spend and a lot of calories into a dumpster fire.

Little indicators of quality are not just noticed by your audience, they are used by Google and other social platforms to rank your content in their search calculus – one of our film production guys advised me a while ago that Google penalizes commonly available video clips and rewards the use of higher value, and higher cost, stock footage.

It stopped me from cheaping out and while our client had to bite the bullet, the results were fantastic. ROI results.

If you hadn't noticed directly, the NFL has increased the number of cameras involved in a game from 3 back in 2015, to 20 today. And, if you pay attention next time you watch, you will see what a ginormous difference it makes in overall quality and production values.

The NFL stopped simply recording games and started creating cinematic stories from game footage shot in real-time – when we pull all of that B-roll and dice it into promos and commercials, we can see measurable payoffs immediately.

Want to be different? Want to create high-quality content that folks will watch? Want to demonstrate you have the smarts and courage to challenge the machine?

Want to succeed?

> The task is not so much to see what no one has yet seen; but to think what nobody has yet thought, about that which everybody sees.
>
> ~ Erwin Schrodinger

BRAND AUTHORITY/BRAND AWARENESS/BRANDED CONTENT

More emphasis on brand awareness and authority and less on low-converting lead gen campaigns will provide sales uplift in the future, as buyers are increasingly seeking entertainment and information and they value those elements over feature and function. With the average number of point-solution tools installed today exceeding 70, the IT environment is nobody's first rodeo.

Buyers will buy based on factors we are not considering.

That shift will require bold courage on behalf of our marketers who will need to brave the results of ripping up yesterday's scripts and pioneering paths away from the thinking box. We are optimistic and confident that the future will see a movement toward broadening awareness across a wide band of demographics, as more and more breaches hammer IT and target industrial control systems that manage the distribution of essential consumer products like food, water, and energy.

Regular citizens are now in the game and they need to align with companies who express values they respect.

What we do and how we do it, in both cybersecurity marketing and in cybersecurity defense, will be directional signals for both progress and regress in the years to come. The devil is in the details and there are many moving parts to these puzzles, but putting stakes in the ground for both how we defend (Zero Trust) and how we move markets (alternate messaging on alternate media channels), is a good place to start.

BRANDED CONTENT

One of the highest impact techniques for audience reach in crowded spaces like cybersecurity markets in the coming months is branded content – there are now over 5000 companies competing for attention in this market – same buyers – same message.

A classic example is Apple's *The Morning Show* with Jennifer Aniston and Steve Carrell. It was created by Apple for Apple and features their products in a way that highlights their diversity and integration into everyday life.

But, what is it exactly?

First, branded content doesn't focus on products and services. Instead, there is greater focus on more abstract values and brand story.

It's not invasive. Banner ads and digital formats force audience to pay attention. Branded content is consumed voluntarily. It seeks to attract audience naturally and bring them in.

It generates an emotional connection. Branded content tells stories that excite an audience. Compare static, pre-programmed, and moderated discussions with a sponsor's SME to experts engaging in dialog over a topic that highlights a brand's offerings.

The settings imply genuine, open forums for the exploration of a technology solution by topical experts. The brand is never mentioned.

The emotional connection associates the brand with a solution, and the audience remembers it for a long time. Think the Masters Golf tournament and IBM.

Branded content can be produced in sharable formats which lead to social network virality.

It dramatically improves the positioning of the brand.

Because it tells a story that represents the values associated with the brand, the audience takes away an impression of positive impact.

Because it generates engagement and loyalty, it can provoke a response at a much deeper level and eventually becomes part of its customer identity.

It can promote traffic and leads. A well-produced branded content campaign will bring traffic to your website and will fill the top of your conversion funnel.

The *Morning Show* took Apple's game over the top in the face of strong competition from Android devices.

The stakes were high.

Apple recognized what needed to be done and acted.

The result? Back on top.

Comparing your cybersecurity brand today to mega-brands like Apple may seem impossible. But, it is not. It wasn't too long ago that I was awestruck watching a fellow train passenger page through her new Apple phone. Creating compelling branded content and buying placement is far less expensive than you might imagine - streaming and economies of scale have worked their magic - and many futurists now predict the era of broadcast TV to be ended by 2030.

From RedBull, to Honeywell to Broadcom to Rockwell to Cybereason, the examples abound.

There is a reason cybersecurity marketers have latched on.

It works.

We now have a conveyer belt of advertising designed apparently to answer questions we don't have with brand promises they can't keep, all trying to capture their buyers' attention and push a weak signal through a stubborn wall of noise.

Is it working?

No.

Your brand should capture your business purpose, values, and meaning, and creating branded content is one of the most effective ways you can express these qualities and, expand your reach.

The goal of advertising is to push your message to as many people as possible regardless of their interest in the messaging, product, service, or how well you have defined your target personas.

Today, even folks who should be interested, aren't interested.

To capture those targets, we need to stop selling.

Gasp!

Instead, we need to make people fall in love with our brands.

Branded content is the opposite of traditional advertising. It is based on brand stories that matter to people and then the connective media that associates the stories with the brand values. You don't have to figure out how to connect those values to your products or services. Your audience will do it themselves.

The branded content approach turns traditional marketing methods on their heads by eliminating content that delivers immediate benefits and interests.

Gasp! [again]

But if you look at the empirical data and think about it objectively, you will see plainly that CISOs and other influencers share some characteristics that are not in harmony with your conventional messaging:

- They already understand everything you are trying to explain to them so they quickly tune you and your messaging out;

- They have no time to read stuff and no patience for stuff that sounds like everyone else's stuff;

- They are insulted when companies boast that their product "leverages our proprietary vector-fencing technology to protect every attack surface from the bad guys," and it always seemed to us that insulting your prospect was not a great way to approach marketing;

- They know that your charts and graphs favor your solution or you wouldn't be using them, so they ignore your carefully wrought statistical evidence of superiority.

So, what DO they want?

- An understanding of who you are and what you stand for; your values;

- To be entertained, but in useful ways;

- They want stories and they expect high production values;

- They DON'T want quotidian Zoom rooms where obvious product pushers stand embarrassingly close to their messaging.

They want great stories. Told by credible people and peers, not sales guys. They want something to believe in and something that they can take to their board with confidence that they have made the right decision.

The stakes are so high now, and the competition so fierce that innovative product companies are not being heard or covered by the press and their solutions are being threatened by a frantic, yet unfulfilled, need to get their message to market. We need to slow down and let our buyers absorb our essence and our solution within a context of trust – we need connection first so we can build confidence on our buyer's behalf which will give them permission to make a purchase decision with you.

The buyer benefits, you benefit, and, more importantly, our industry benefits by bringing a new technology solution into the fold that will raise the bar for intruders.

WHAT'S NEXT?

As we have pointed out, exploitation of the open-source supply chain will accelerate a continuation of today's supply chain/ransomware attacks, and an increase in both fiscal demands and frequency.

We should prepare for a large-scale Industrial Control attack, designed similarly to that of Petya/NotPetya, and released in the wild to test another self-directed attack of massive proportion.

We will likely continue the frustratingly slow progress we are making toward a public and private cybersecurity defense union, impacted by conflicting political agendas, internal squabbling, and hierarchical directives along with increased and emboldened rhetoric from both Russia and China.

Both countries will continue to flex their newly affirmed cyber superiority with fresh global threats and expanded disruption.

The next few months will expose more point-solution competition from a collective of new players in the cybersecurity marketplace. Much of this competition will be fueled by large injections of venture capital into startups and early-stage companies bringing AI and ML technologies to the automated detection and defense stage.

The $45 million series B rounds had been unheard of, even in the heady days of 2020, yet they have become commonplace today; and $250 million investments in spin-offs like VisibleRisk to BitSight by Moody's and Team8, position incomplete, though popular Board-level solutions serve as front-runners in the race for huge-value IPOs or acquisition.

Sometime later this year, we will see what happens when China announces a quantum crypto break that will demonstrate breaking the traditional public key crypto.

Work-from-home (WFH) and borderless perimeter threats will continue to reveal new problems exacerbating a continuing trend into the coming year and beyond, like the data coming out of every study about the reliability and dependability of VPNs.

More discovery will continue to showcase an increase in scope and complexity.

More complexity, confusion, and chaos.

As more people have adopted the WFH protocols, employees will take cybersecurity shortcuts for convenience, and insufficiently secured personal devices and routers, along with the transfer of sensitive information over unsecured or unsanctioned channels, will continue to serve as an accelerant for data breaches and leaks.

We will need and might see, a stronger emphasis on detection of cybersecurity threats in the next two years, as we all now know that protection alone has not defeated the biggest and most damaging cybersecurity threats in history.

Advanced, unified, and extended detection and response vendors should see a majority of the spotlight in the next few months in concert with another hybrid virtual RSAC (the RSA Conference) – the biggest cybersecurity convention in the world, now presenting on a combination phsyical and virtual platform. It appeared to lose about 60% of its normal physical traffice according to local reports, then RSA sold the entire show to Symphony Technology Group, a Private Equity firm who hasn't yet announced the conditions around next year's show. Visibility, detection, and response, when it comes to threats characterized by unprecedented levels of sophistication, professionalism, and maliciousness, will dominate the market.

We may also see an increase in the adoption of AI-based and machine learning Cloud SIEM tools, and an increase in automated threat hunting and orchestration in real-time, providing that more granular visibility so important to early threat detection.

Or, we may remain so busy fighting off big, incoming threats that we won't have time to address and/or properly assess any new technologies, regardless of promise.

As Mark Twain said, "The future interests me, as I am going to spend the rest of my life there."

Indeed.

CHAPTER 7

Why We Got Here

W e now know how we got here. The question is why we got
here.

When all of this began back in the early 2000s with the advent of a
connected world, the entire business community was so enamored with
the opportunity to replace manual processes with electronic equivalents,
we focused only on the path toward digitalization and electronic
commerce.

When business units said jump, we said how high? When they said
move, we said how fast?

I know quite well, because my companies were happy contributors to
the gold rush.

A LITTLE HISTORY

Prior to our acquisition by seeCommerce, VIT had been a lead player in
the Data Warehouse information delivery space, enabling large, enterprise
companies to create actionable information out of huge chunks of data
stored in giant data lakes. I served as Founding VP, Sales and Marketing.

As a part of seeCommerce, we became a key puzzle piece in the
conversion of legacy data to useful analytics that helped determine the
efficacy of e-commerce programs and prior to seeCommerce's acquisition by Teradata, helped the company become a leader in the supply
chain performance management segment.

Our flagship product helped companies align strategies and operations, and identify opportunities for improvement, allowing business

DOI: 10.1201/9781003331773-8

managers and executives to see and collaborate across the total supply chain to measure, monitor, and exceed supply chain performance objectives, for example, optimizing for electronic commerce along the way.

We did so, without a thought to data security or Internet security which, following the advent of the Internet, became known as cybersecurity.

INFORMATION TECHNOLOGY MEETS DESIGN

USWeb had been one of North America's first fully fledged Internet agencies, founded in 1995 by a group of former Novell software employees. Run by CEO Joseph Firmage with backing from a variety of venture capital groups, the company spent most of 1996 buying up a variety of small interactive agencies around the United States to create a national network. The following year USWeb went public, and used the additional funds to purchase network services group Gray Peak and digital design agency CKS.

The latter was the brainchild of three former Apple employees.

Bill Cleary left Apple in 1987 to set up a marketing company called Cleary Communications, producing multimedia presentations for his former employers. He was joined over the next two years by former colleagues Mark Kvamme and Tom Suiter, whose initials (CKS) gave the business its new name in 1991.

USWeb's focus had been entirely on helping companies get on the Internet and change their business models from the physical world to the world of online commerce, and all of the promotional and support messaging underneath that movement.

No one had any reason throughout the 1990s and early 2000s to consider threats or exposures to an ecosystem that was rapidly expanding in the shadows to engulf the Internet as a backbone for business. No one had attacked anyone, and I do not ever recall any board room conversations about cybersecurity, data privacy, loss, or leakage during that entire period.

The merger of USWeb and CKS in 1997 created what was at the time America's biggest interactive agency, and one of the country's top-20 marketing groups. The subsequent merger of Whittman-Hart and USWeb/CKS was completed at the very beginning of March 2000, giving rise to the new corporate name of marchFIRST.

Merging Whittman-Hart's software systems and consultancy business with USWeb/CKS's strategic and design offering, the business had a huge portfolio of digital and e-business skills, enjoyed combined revenue of more than $1bn, and employed more than 8500 people in 70 offices and 14 countries worldwide.

With the crash of 2000, marchFIRST ended badly, announcing losses of $73 million in two quarters and saw the exit of folks like Bob Bernard, the founder of Whittman-Hart and a quick bankruptcy filing rendering my ton of stock acquired at $30/share virtually valueless at 6 cents each.

Prior to the crash, I had left marchFIRST to start my own version of CKS/USWeb.

THE 2000S

My business, known at the time as Endymion Systems, grew rapidly and attracted a $15m "A" round of venture capital from investors like Draper Fischer's MeVC $300 million fund, growing crazily to 285 people and four branch offices, with annually recurring revenues of $48 million by the end of our first year. We were able to attract clients like Nike, Abercrombie & Fitch, mPower (now Morningstar), and Harley Davidson for whom we built lifestyle businesses online – none of which were threatened by changes in market values or even a hint of cybersecurity risk.

When the Internet reached broad adoption in 2002, however, an interesting confluence of events revealed a sudden increase in the appearance of worms, viruses, and Internet-facing vulnerability exploits, which gave rise to an attention shift toward these potential threats to data privacy and transactional integrity within e-commerce.

During the 1970s and 1980s, most information technology processing was limited to academia and mainframe or client-server computing, both limited to only physical relationships between users and data. Users submitted batches of punched cards or later online entries through TSO on the mainframe to move data in and out of mostly single processors.

In fact, I along with the aforementioned Shawn McLaren and the Cambridge Systems Group company we co-founded, brought only the second data security product to market to compete with the IBM version which was used strictly to guarantee data integrity stored on mainframe computers. If it weren't for corporate auditors, the Department of

Defense (DoD) and the The National Security Agency (NSA) as later learned, even that level of security would not have been approached.

Sometimes legislation and compliance mandates are useful.

THE DoD AND NSA STEP IN WHERE ANGELS DARE TO TREAD

It wasn't that some congressional legislation had emerged from committee with the brilliant idea that data should be secured, but rather that the DoD in 1980 decided that all U.S. data centers must be able to provide proven and established data security practices within its data processing facilities and issued voluminous guidelines and requirements for auditors to use to create and execute examination standards.

These standards, as specified in the DoD Trusted Computer System Evaluation Criteria, DoD 5200.28-STD (also known as TCSEC or the Orange Book), applied also, but not limited, to the computer systems in companies working with a government contract. The criteria corresponded to a particular security designation, depending on the type and amount of security the system provides. The security designations ranged from D (the least amount of security) through C1, C2, B1, B2, B3, and A1.

The NSA was trained to perform a formal evaluation to determine whether a data processing system adhered to the guidelines and requirements for a given security designation and would work hand-in-hand with corporate audit departments to assure that the protocols were in force. This attention was disguised under the umbrella of advanced scrutiny ahead of looming global threats for capturing employee information whether from private or public company employees or agencies of the U.S. Federal government and their employees.

The NSA's actual and far more sinister role in the origination and fostering of these rules and standards falls into crisp focus as we learn more about the their quietly expanding role in cybersecurity over time.

CHAPTER 8

The Institutionalization

N otwithstanding the Morris worm of 1988, at the moment when the Internet began to demonstrate its unbounded connectivity and use-cases in e-commerce and online transactions, far more practical computer viruses and network intrusions began to take off as well.

After the spread of viruses in the 1990s, the 2000s marked the institutionalization of cyber threats and cybersecurity.

One could argue, in fact, that the real beginnings of cybersecurity awareness in the commercial world got its kick start in 2002, when Lawrence A. Gordon and Martin P. Loeb published a paper, in *ACM Transactions on Information and System Security*, entitled "The Economics of Information Security Investment." What became known as The Gordon–Loeb model is a mathematical economic framework that provides the formulation upon which an analysis in the optimal investment level in information security can be developed.

Thus began the organizational acknowledgment in the world of commerce that threats from cyber-related activities were having some sort of impact on traditional information systems in the commercial world.

But, behind the green curtain, the National Security Agency was operating the digital levers that were leading to a global spike in Internet-related malware attacks in the 1990s, created by cyber-criminals who had permitted themselves to attack U.S. firms based on vectors developed by the NSA to spy and disrupt the national defense programs of our adversaries.

Which is why, in the late 1990s, we saw a sudden increase in cyber-attacks in the world of global commerce. Where did this new toy come from?

ALL'S FAIR IN LOVE AND WAR

The official charter of the NSA was to guard and protect U.S. information systems and collect foreign intelligence. Protecting information systems includes evaluating software, for the purpose of identifying security flaws, then taking steps to correct the flaws. By definition, a defensive motion.

Collecting intelligence depends upon exploiting security flaws to extract information, which is an offensive motion and has been in play in one form or another in warfare since the beginning of time.

The Internet arrived and dumped rocket fuel on the NSA engine.

Companies and governments around the world use commonly available commercial products for operational purposes, many of which come from Microsoft. The NSA, in order to become prolific at intelligence collection, develop code that can penetrate the native defenses of these products and extract information protected by their defensive shields. The more these vulnerabilities are discovered and exploited, the better and more useful the intelligence the NSA can gather becomes.

So, as you might imagine, these discoveries are never reported to the Microsoft's of the world nor are they publicized to the tens of million+ users who are dependent upon these same products for their day-to-day business operations.

In other words, the correction of these security flaws makes the flaws unavailable for NSA exploitation, and is thus counter-productive to one of their primary missions, yet as a by-product, guarantees that the backbone software systems we depend on for running our businesses are full of exploitable flaws.

Many, both inside and external to the cybersecurity community, believe that this un-addressed scenario also defines insanity and since we have all been aware of it since the beginning, we're all responsible for the outcome. Whosoever is responsible, one can use that moment as the starting point for the amplified cybersecurity spiral in which we find ourselves today.

Eventually, of course, through the early and mid-2000s, other nations, and most noticeably Russia, Iran, North Korea, and China had acquired their own offensive capability, and enjoyed using it against the United States.

As a former skinny kid who was kicked around the playground and discovered Jack Lalanne's Power Juice; then gleefully returned to take it to the bullies s/he once feared, so too did those nation-states, who for years had operated within the shadow of the American global military strength, find new strength and cybersecurity parity and often superiority in the exploitation of these common flaws.

By 2016, our own hacking tools were regularly being used against us by Russia and North Korea. This new and potentially deadly global competition set off a flurry of recruitment activity where NSA employees and contractors were being wooed with high salaries and mega-perks by our adversaries.

Patriots or not, everyone apparently has a price.

THE CISO ERA BEGINS

Revenge campaigns began to blossom and in 2007, the United States and Israel began a joint exercise that exploited security flaws in the Microsoft Windows operating system to attack and damage equipment used by Iran to refine nuclear materials. Iran responded, not by offering a cease and desist, but rather by escalating their own cyberwarfare offensive pressure, focused specifically on the United States and Israel.

Thus, by the mid-2000s, a few short years after the introduction of the Internet, cybersecurity became a reality and a risk element for all organizations depending on the web for information sharing and e-commerce.

Our colleagues on the business and commercial side of the fence were somewhat isolated from the sharpest end of the spears and continued building and expanding their information technology backbone almost as if nothing had happened to threaten it. It wasn't that our leaders didn't recognize the risks a cyber threat presented, it was their view that it was simply inconceivable that it would happen to them or that it could take their operations down to the extent that it would threaten their livelihood.

Based on the Gordon–Loeb model, they could calculate to the contrary.

But cyber-attacks began to occur and their targets were medium and small businesses, academia, healthcare, manufacturing, finserv, retail, and government. The dark web was morphing into an ancient bazaar-style marketplace where anyone could purchase any and all cybersecurity attack tools ranging from exploit kits to insurance, malware, and all of their strains, to pre-packaged attack vectors, keys to open doors and covert access, and lists of vulnerabilities by industrial sector.

Consulting services were available for marketing, advertising, accounting, taxes, website development and design services, and legal interpretations of international law. Whatever a cyber-criminal needs to become a player, we got it and you can buy it.

In an attempt to both combat and prepare for this new world, the era of the titular role of Chief Information Security Officer was born and the fight over reporting relationship and authority began in earnest. Many CISOs believed that they should report directly to the CEO and many CEOs thought the function should report instead directly to the Chief Financial Officer or the CIO or even to a committee made up of senior corporate officers and an occasional board member.

At the same time, commercial enterprises began wondering how they might determine risk handling within this new threat envelope because, as they well might have, they saw cybersecurity risk as just another of its kind, no more or less significant than the physical and psychological risks with which board members routinely deal.

Enabled by the Gordon–Loeb model, and much to the confusion and chagrin of CISOs, companies were clamoring for a safe rationale with which to deal with the cybersecurity threat. In addition to investing in new technologies, people and processes to combat the increasing cyber-attacks, companies were choosing to absorb and/or transfer some or all of the risk as part of their ERM process.

ISOLATING ROI

Investing new funds to protect company data involves a class of cost that, unlike other investments, is not intended to grow revenue, generate new profit, or accrete to the EBITDA performance. It is simply seen as a necessary expense required to prevent additional costs. Thus, a model like that of Gordon–Loeb, is useful in isolating the specific expense required to protect a set of data, as well as the potential loss in the event the data is stolen, damaged, or corrupted.

Driving the model, requires that the company understand, quantitatively

1. what the data is worth;

2. the extent to which the data is at risk; and

3. the probability of a successful attack on the data.

These three parameters become the calculus that identifies the median money loss with no additional security investment.

Historically, that model generally produced results that underscored the fact that the actual money a company would have to spend to protect the information at risk should be only a small fraction of the predicted loss value. In case after case, the model said that investments in cybersecurity or computer security-related activities for amounts higher than 37% of the predicted loss would always turn negative.

In fact, the calculus got quickly apprehended by laws of diminishing returns along the way.

For example, companies saw that they can enjoy greater economic returns by investing in cyber and information security technology, people, and processes aimed to increase the security of data sets with a medium level of vulnerability, than by doing the same thing with data that is highly vulnerable.

In other words, an early indicator of one of the principles of Zero Trust that suggests protecting high value and critical assets, regardless of vulnerability and focusing on the vulnerabilities later.

Here's some math:

You have data valued at $5,000,000, with an attack probability of 12%, and a 75% chance that an attack would be successful.

The potential loss in this case is $450,000 ($5,000,000 × 0.12 × 0.75 = $450,000).

According to the Gordon–Loeb model, the company's investment should not exceed $450,000 × 0.37 or $166,500.

In modern cybersecurity spend, $166,500 doesn't buy too much.

Objective analytics like these are the culprit behind the rejection of the CISO's eternal request for additional funding for cybersecurity programs and the vast majority of CISOs who fail to understand this reality also fail to understand the small role they actually play in the grand economic scheme.

When you are under constant attack and you are the General, it is easy to get caught up in the notion of indispensability relative to your role.

Were CISOs told for instance that their role was to simply make sure the lights came on every day and that their employer were kept out of the headlines, they would be shocked. But that is often the way they are seen by senior C-suite and board members.

As a former CISO, I don't relish in sharing that knowledge, nor do I agree in total that the role of the CISO should be this diminished. I will expand soon on why that is, why it has been ignored, and why the overall increase in risk and exploitable vulnerability has been the outcome.

IT AND OT: A NARROWED VISION

Part of the dilemma is that along the way to an increasing less secure environment, virtually every commercial enterprise has rigorously ignored the operational technology side of the house, and in addition to pipes, valves, and sensors, believed that late-entry smart devices like refrigerators, micro-wave ovens, and coffeemakers in break rooms and cameras, access control devices, landscape controls, and lighting scattered around the campus along with polycom and similar devices networked into conference rooms, were immune from cyber-takeover and network penetration.

Leadership also believed that because the OT plant network that was controlling our factory automation through SCADA and ICS devices were safely air-gapped away from our corporate enterprise networks upon which we stored all of our critical information assets, electronic processing, and communications between and among our internal employees and our external partners and employees working in remote locations, we were safe from unlawful access, vandalism, or breach.

We also failed to recognize that the pipes and valves and sensors controlling the flow of product to our customers were sort of important and that we couldn't afford to leave them to the fates decided by an undeclared information security leadership role with responsibility for the outcome and authority over the protection protocols, but with no charter to execute the corrections and preventions necessary to harden them to cyber-attacks.

THE TECHNOLOGY OF A NEW ERA

We failed to notice as local area networks morphed into wide area networks into SASE, into the Edge, and the Cloud and the underlying technology changing almost monthly for the past 20 years, all responding to faster chips and faster, broader bandwidth, and a move to software defined everything, new open-systems protocols, libraries and configurations, micro-segmentations, Dockers and containers revolutionizing software development, and dramatic reductions in size and increases in power enabling our hand-held phones to operate as fully functional computing devices that would shame their predecessors of the middle 90s.

If I told you that in 1975, a half Meg of RAM for a 370/155 computer cost $250,000, your mind couldn't find a place to hold or process that data, but that is exactly where we stood less than 50 years ago.

So, grabbing the year 2020, we find ourselves locked into a computing era paradigm that rewards speed to market, insane growth and scale, and new products defining new categories, previously unknown and unseen threats that now represent risk to our infrastructure of unprecedented varieties.

Once the Internet became the mule upon whose back we gained passage to faster, better computing, our entire CIO community from the smallest of shops down in Cape Girardeau, Missouri, to shining mega-institutions like JPMorgan Chase's fabulous equipped and resourced data centers in Delaware and New Jersey, began to accept requests from business units to produce new business systems to assist them in their own growth initiatives.

When Gates stumbled into IBM in the late 70s and created the IBM PC, he did so with software he coerced out of a guy named Gary Kildall, known for creating the first-ever operating system, the Control Program for Microcomputers, or CPM. Or, so the story goes. Gary was a computer scientist, holding a degree in Mathematics and a Ph.D. in Computer Science, and had an already established company, Digital Research Incorporated (DRI).

Gates met Kildall through an introduction by IBM and Kildall and after a long planning session. a subsequent meeting was set between Kindall and IBM to discuss the future OS of this new consumer gadget computer. Bill strongly encouraged Kindall to attend and close through happy visions of market dominance and millionaire status, to say nothing of a senior position of authority at Bill's new company, Microsoft.

Kindall, who was more of an inventor than a businessman, didn't take Bill's advice too seriously and forgot about the meeting - was out flying one of his private planes when IBM showed up at his doorstep.

Seeing he wasn't home, they proceeded to pressure his wife, Dorothy, to sign an NDA stating that IBM was never here. She refused. Feeling angry and frustrated, they returned to Bill Gates and pressed him again to see if Microsoft could develop an OS for the IBM PC. Bill was not about to give Gary a second chance and he accepted the deal.

But here's what Gates did first: he bought a program from a small software company called the Quick and Dirty Operating System (or Q-DOS), for $75,000. Q-DOS was, in fact, an earlier ripoff of Gary's CPM program which he had shared with them for some inexplicable reason. He then changed its name to MS-DOS (Microsoft DOS) and licensed it to IBM. A year later, IBM's personal computers entered the market and MS-DOS was sold alongside each one of them.

Realizing what Microsoft had done, Gary threatened to sue IBM for copyright infringement. This prompted the company to strike a deal with him and DRI: CPM would now be offered for sale alongside MS-DOS. The terms seemed fair and Gary was satisfied: customers could now choose which operating system they wanted on their machine.

But Gary had once again missed the small print: It was true that CPM was offered to customers alongside MS-DOS, but while MS-DOS sold for $40, CPM sold for $240. This price discrepancy caused CPM's death. Now, Gary Killdal is remembered mostly for being "the man who could've been Bill Gates". Take at least one business class alongside your PhD program in Cybersecurity. Just in case.

Suddenly, the world of information technology became accessible to the person on the street. Now we had applications that would serve users outside of accounting, manufacturing, and engineering and regular folks began to understand what was happening above those raised floors. Now we had two large information channels, home and business computing, each used for different things, yet each relied upon the Internet to get them there.

We subsequently added gaming, streaming, online education; and packaged small business applications and technologies that would allow PCs and/or iPhones to connect with mainframe computers to digital conduct life, from banking to mortgage loan applications, from DIY how-to's to travel planning, online shopping, and medical exams.

Suddenly, our personal computers and iPhones became business-centric devices as well, providing convenient end-point devices for information and activity sharing, application processing, and connectivity portals through which we could stay connected to fellow workers via email, Zoom, Chat, Teams, Signal, and Slack, as well as a myriad of business applications, like Payroll, Sales, and ERP.

But while all of this was exploding, the conventional backbones that supported all of the new horsepower, switching, and routing requirements were not being replaced with bigger, faster, more mature versions. Why?

One of the main reasons is we don't have back-up power generators locked into our power grids.

Not only do we use the same network infrastructure backbone designs that served us well in the late 1990s, we have completely ignored the critical infrastructure upon which our daily lives here in digital and analog reality depend upon for subsistence.

It was as if we could not say no.

As a CIO in the early days, I can attest to that inability. Saying no to business growth was simply not an option, though to be honest, I never considered it.

Why?

I was the guy, and my ego siad yes - I will build this thing and get us to the next level. A legend in my own mind.

And every significant change in business requirements led to increases in network complexity that should have resulted in a rip and replace with a new and business-appropriate network topology designed to accommodate whatever shift in computing paradigm was implied – mainframes to distributed client-server to cloud computing on the edge – we did not.

Instead of building new networks, we layered on changes.

Why?

Because it was easy, fast, and cost-efficient. We relied upon our classically untrained network technicians to provide fixes and patches and workarounds to accommodate new requirements and document those changes for the next generation of network support folks who had to understand what went on historically to divine the modifications required for future accommodations.

But documentation as is often the case, got lost in the shuffle and we subsequently did the best we could with what we knew and produced workarounds for what we didn't.

What began in 1973 as an Ethernet network developed like many things in computer technology in the Xerox Labs in Palo Alto, became standardized in 1974 by the publication of the Transmission Control

Protocol (TCP) specification, ominously coining the word Internet as an abbreviation for internetworking.

By 1998, Ethernet supported transmission speeds of 1 Gbit/s (Gigabytes per second) and then higher speeds of up to 400 Gbit/s were added (as of 2018). The scaling of the Ethernet has been a key enabling factor to its continued use as well as its continued contribution to our inability to defend against advanced cyber threats.

WORRY LATER

Speed kills, and it is the enemy of all CISOs everywhere.

It seems that the cycle of innovation in telecommunications occurs roughly every ten years and in our modern world, it frequently shows up in the release of the next generation of mobile communication networks, bringing faster speeds and increased capabilities.

Back in ancient times, the first-generation (1G) wireless network enabled the first cell phones. Then, ten years later, 2G brought improved coverage and texting, while 3G introduced voice with data/Internet ten years later, and 4G/4G long-term evolution (LTE) ultimately delivered dramatically increased speeds to keep up with mobile data demand.

Today, 5G technology looms right around the corner and promises to completely transform telecommunication networks, with 100-times-faster download speeds, 10-times decrease in latency, enabling new capabilities, such as remote surgery and autonomous, self-driving cars, and near-infinitely increased network capacity, allowing millions of devices to be connected to the same network within a small geo-footprint.

In addition, 5G will pave the way for additional new capabilities and will support connectivity for applications like smart homes and cities, industrial automation, autonomous vehicles, telemedicine, and virtual/augmented reality.

Our former CISA Director, Chris Krebs has said that, "From my perspective, 5G is the single biggest critical infrastructure build that the globe has seen in the last 25 years and, coupled with the growth of cloud computing, automation, and future of artificial intelligence, demands focused attention today to secure tomorrow."

He is absolutely right and it should scare the hell out of everyone. In fact, it is the poster-child for why we got here.

Initial 5G deployments will operate on existing 4G and 4G-LTE infrastructure and non-standalone 4G/5G hybrid infrastructures. In spite of messaging to the contrary, the complete evolution to standalone 5G networks is likely years away. In the meantime, the goal of 5G is to meet the increasing data and communication requirements of personal computing and business applications through these non-standalone networks, all while proving these amazing 5G benefits, safely and securely.

I love 5G, because it so clearly illustrates what goes wrong and why it goes wrong. It is not just the poster-child, it is a textbook lesson in how we got here and why we got here. If there were a branded blanket we could wrap ourselves in, the slogan would be, "We'll Worry Later."

Network complexity and telecommunication speed will combine to fire the last few nails into the coffin of cybersecurity, proving a fitting finish to the earlier work done by our government agencies corrupting the software systems upon which we run our businesses without bothering to notify us about the threats and vulnerabilities now inherent in those products, our fascination with open-source code and APIs for connectivity to anything, and our attraction toward shiny new technology solutions.

By the mid-2000s, we were fully cooked and fried and ready for prime time.

Though we continued to increase our knowledge of the threat landscape, the vulnerabilities inherent in our core backbone products, the best practices that encouraged hygiene in patch and configuration management, our attempts at controlled cloud entry, our processes for Digital Forensics and Incident Response (DFIR), and our ability to stand-up functioning SOCs.

We may not have been great at DevSecOps, but we tried. We looked to NIST, MITRE, and OWASP for guidance. We looked to eLearning platforms to upskill our troops. We looked to recruitment to accelerate our hiring of now-critical resources. We looked everywhere we could and lifted up every suspicious rock we could find, but we still could not keep up with the global demand for the same resources or contract the skills gap, or dent the resource challenge in any meaningful way.

THE SKILLS GAP

As a CIO, I understood the requirement limitations of ERP systems quite well and the possibilities for extensions and creative enablement beyond their design became a personal challenge. My users in process and design engineering who worked on disc substrates, communication terminals, disc dives and ultimately mini-computers had a much better handle on the limitations of the resource pool under my direction and insisted they do their own programming, development, and even systems operation on the mainframes that fell under my watch.

My brain wrapped around the complexities of process manufacturing and I respected their view of a world that was very different than IT. In fact, as I compared their resources to my own, engineering resources trained in the rigors of product development and testing, it was clear to me that qualifying as a Professional Design Engineer required a skill set and disciplines well above those of my development teams.

My teams got their degrees in cubicles writing COBOL and RPG code to automate simple discreet processes that were unaffected by complications from environmental controls and changes in current and amplitude. Writing a program to update a payroll record with a new name and address field is a little different than writing code that would solve for the automation of sequencing priorities for multiple thick, thin, web, and mobile run-time clients connected to a main SCADA server hub over an internal Ethernet-based network.

And this incredible disconnect is another major contributing factor to the question of why we got here.

The first computer science department in the United States was formed at Purdue University in 1962, yet what originated and followed had great trouble getting out of its own way for years. Edsger Dijkstra, a Dutch theoretical physicist and computer scientist correctly opined that "computer science is no more about computers than astronomy is about telescopes."

The design and deployment of computers and computer systems is generally considered the province of disciplines other than computer science.

The study of computer hardware is usually considered part of computer engineering, while the study of commercial computer systems and their deployment is often called information technology or information systems.

While Computer Studies has been taught in U.K. schools going back to 1981, it only recently became a compulsory part of the National Curriculum. In 2014, it became an educational entitlement for all pupils over the age of 4.

Yet, the medicine must not have taken hold as the United Kingdom leads most of the western world in breaches. Sorry, mates, just saying.

In 2008, 14,000 U.S. school districts joined in a common effort to decide upon a computer science curriculum via teacher committee;

development was fractured. The Association for Computing Machinery (ACM) and Computer Science Teachers Association (CSTA) issued a progress report that claimed only 14 out of 50 states had adopted significant education standards for high school computer science.

Debate raged over emphasis and program direction but all involved agreed that Mathematics must become a key component in any Computer Science degree. As a former Math major, I believe I am entitled to my opinion that differential equations matter not a whit in the prosecution of todays applied computer science challenges.

Except in OT cybersecurity, which is yet a thing.

My hiring and vetting process at IBM was determined by passing a two-page set of math "problems" that anyone in the 6th grade at the time could have nailed (Arithmetic operations, negative numbers, properties of numbers, variables and expressions, equations and inequalities, and geometry) even in U.S. public schools.

The degrees that eventually emerged from all of this study, research, testing, and debate focused too heavily on math and regulatory compliance issues and too lightly on the core metabolism of advanced threats and the processes required to build functional defenses. In other words, we were graduating administrators when what we sorely needed were warriors.

While computer science degrees approached ubiquity long after I retired from CIO practice, the current approach to learning paths and curriculum miss most of the point, and if being positioned as foundational for cybersecurity, they are not well targeted in their content. The mis-fire might be best represented by the approach to programming training.

In academia, many calories are dedicated to the primary programming languages, in spite of the fact that only service-oriented programming, the programming paradigm that uses "services" as the unit of computer work, to design and implement integrated business applications and mission critical software programs, is truly applicable to the actual work whether in software development or cybersecurity utility.

And most software development is now done by combining prior work taken from open-source libraries, representing processing routines in common use, and APIs which provide access and connective tissue to other software or data structures as part of the new development code.

Most all open-source software and APIs are dependent upon other open-source modules that will be called at execution time, and it is virtually impossible to control the processes that result.

Under-resourcing provides the excuse for failure to vet even the direct open-source code, let alone the dependent code, so most often new code included native and unpatched vulnerabilities within existing code and APIs. But under-resourcing is never matched by under-requirements or under-expectations.

Move and Jump.

A recent SlashData survey tell us that 90% of developers regularly use open-source code in their software development work and that the number of active global developers has grown to 23.6 million.

In their Developer Economics survey, reaching more than 17,000 developers globally, SlashData found that 89% of them regularly used APIs and that the majority (69%) of them used open-source APIs.

So, we have Computer Science classes focusing on programming languages that are largely irrelevant, stressing administrator functionality which is unnecessary within the workload gap, emphasizing mathematics which is a field of study both non-essential for the cybersecurity workforce of today, and serves as off-putting as well to a large population of interested and self-taught students, while ignoring rifle and small arms training for those who will become engaged with the enemy in future conflict.

Not enough emphasis on proper upskilling, too much dependency on open-source and vulnerable code, too many classroom hours, and an overly generous contribution to the "why" of how we got here.

CHAPTER 9

The End and the Beginning

I f you are not depressed yet, you haven't been paying attention or you don't care.

I care. Passionately.

And I am not depressed.

In spite of all of the headwinds unleashed by network complexity; transmission speeds; corrupt backbone business software; open-source APIs; supply chain software; inadequate education and upskilling; the gap between resource supply and demand; security awareness training that is poorly designed and infrequently implemented; rapidly growing threats; and adoption of advanced technology by the bad guys, we still have a chance.

We need to address and implement the recommendations outlined in earlier chapters, which by the way, are not the fruit of my own imagination but instead have been contributed over time and long conversations by a couple dozen of the smartest people in cybersecurity defense, who can be found in the acknowledgments.

Taking an unified stand to force the Federal government to join us in active modifications of modern laws and drop the barriers to a truly shared knowledge base is key. That includes transparency with the NSA and any other agency, either developing their own malware or sinking exploits through backdoors in major institutional vendors like Microsoft,

DOI: 10.1201/9781003331773-10

and distributing modified versions of common-use tools and languages like Java.

Then we can do it – then we can make progress toward victory – toward Zero Trust in every shop and boardroom – toward a smarter and more sensitized workforce – toward an unified forward operating base resourced with cooperative forces from government and industry, each sharing what they know – toward automated the vetting of open-source software and APIs – developing an SBOM that will identify our source code structures – automated hygiene for patches and configurations that can be passed through a tool that matches what needs to be done with what we have as fixes – centralization around a suite of proven software and services, validated to provide a core detection and remediation capability – and a fully curated eLearning platform that offers defined, just-in-time course work toward functional and individual certifications and upskilling appropriate to the role.

We need offensive tools and pathways to deliver them – new rules that enable an attack victim to destroy the attacker while inside the network or on the way out – government support for ransomware victims that compensate their mandatory refusal to pay with recovery and re-construction funds within a business operational timeframe – international positioning that encourages cooperation with western countries currently under protection from Russia and the Chinese with extensions of equal and compelling support for food, energy, water, military training, and weaponry and a return to the fundamental principles of NATO – an end to the accommodation of adversarial venture investors and limited partners in funds designed to allow for intimate examination of confidential and proprietary patent data.

Venture capital that targets AI and ML for the automation of today's most tedious, error prone, and consuming manual processes.

These are the stepping stones to get back to a leadership position in cybersecurity.

Epilogue

John Kindervag

Creator of Zero Trust

When I published the first Zero Trust report, "No More Chewy Centers," in 2010, I was a Forrester Analyst tasked with researching the fundamental issues around cybersecurity. Of course, back then, we called it "Information Security," which was, perhaps, a more precise term. (What's a "cyber," and why does it need to be protected?) I was a lone voice back then, more often laughed at than lauded. I could never have imagined that Zero Trust would become a global movement adopted by many massive companies and governmental entities. If you had told me that 11 years later, the President of the United States would endorse Zero Trust through an executive order, I would have advised you to get back in your DeLorean, zoom up to 88 MPH, and go back to Hill City.

The Zero Trust movement didn't happen by itself. It happened because numerous individuals, vendors, and end-users stepped up alongside and agreed that this was a good direction for the cybersecurity industry. Now, Zero Trust adoption is accelerating at an incredible pace. It is a global phenomenon, and I regularly speak with Zero Trust activates from all across the world.

Even a global pandemic hasn't slowed down Zero Trust adoption. COVID-19 has accelerated the enterprise demand for Zero Trust initiatives, as Zero Trust environments, by design, enables a secure remote workforce. Security and business leaders are more aware that most of their employees work outside of the traditional security perimeter and are moving quickly to add Zero Trust architectural and policy controls to their remote access systems.

For me, the pandemic got me off the road and sat me in my office instead of an airplane seat. It allowed me to reengage with people, albeit via video conference, to have substantive conversations about Zero Trust and its future.

One of the most vibrant voices I encountered during my travel respite was Steve King of Cyber Theory. He engaged me in thought-provoking conversations and demonstrated a unique passion for all things Zero Trust. Together we created a Cybersecurity Think Tank – The CyberTheory Institute, which will focus on diving deep into various cybersecurity topics, starting with Zero Trust. Steve has put together an all-star lineup of cyber luminaries to kick off the Institute, and I am forever grateful.

And now, Steve has written a new book on our cybersecurity war and Zero Trust. It is undeniably the best Zero Trust book yet written. While other writers have focused on implementing Zero Trust from their perspectives, Steve focuses on why Zero Trust is so important on the modern cybersecurity battlefield. His concept of the five cyber battlefields is a great insight that will help us win the cyber-war. By weaving Zero Trust principles throughout these five concepts, Steve demonstrates how the ideas and efforts involved in building Zero Trust environments will lead to a profound shift in terrain advantage. No longer will attackers own the high ground. As defenders and protectors, we can leverage modern technology in a Zero Trust way to keep our data and assets safe from exfiltration and exploitation.

I am profoundly grateful to Steve King for writing this book. More than that, however, I am thankful for his friendship, mentorship, guidance, and vision.

John Kindervag, the Creator of Zero Trust
Senior Vice President, Cybersecurity Strategy
ON2IT Group Fellow at ON2IT Cybersecurity
Cofounder of the CyberTheory Institute and the Zero Trust Council
Former Field CTO Palo Alto Networks
Forrester Analyst

Printed in the United States
by Baker & Taylor Publisher Services